HEALING
HIDDEN HURTS

HEALING
HIDDEN HURTS

faith to begin again

RONDA BROWN

DESTINY IMAGE® PUBLISHERS, INC.

P.O. Box 310, Shippensburg, PA 17257-0310

"Speaking to the Purposes of God for This Generation and for the Generations to Come."

This book and all other Destiny Image, Revival Press, MercyPlace, Fresh Bread, Destiny Image Fiction, and Treasure House books are available at Christian bookstores and distributors worldwide.

For a U.S. bookstore nearest you, call 1-800-722-6774.
For more information on foreign distributors, call 717-532-3040.
Or reach us on the Internet: www.destinyimage.com.

ISBN 10: 0-7684-3109-3
ISBN 13: 978-0-7684-3109-4

For Worldwide Distribution, Printed in the U.S.A.

1 2 3 4 5 6 7 8 9 10 11 / 13 12 11 10 09

DEDICATION

This book is gratefully dedicated to my One True Love, the One who holds me when I cry and laughs with me when I laugh, my Eternal Love: Jesus. Through Him and the Holy Spirit, I have experienced goodness and eternal mercy beyond what I ever deserved. His unending love has been so prevalent throughout my life; I would sincerely be lost without Him.

-Jesus my Beautiful Darling-

I worship You as my Savior,

I honor You as my King,

I love You as my Father,

I treasure You as my Friend!

AUTHOR'S NOTE

This book represents an actual and detailed account of my testimony, and the lessons I have learned. The names of some of the people have been changed to ensure their impunity and privacy.

ACKNOWLEDGMENTS

To my precious children, who gave me the will to survive. The Lord used you both greatly as a living example of His goodness to me.

To my sister, Brandi, whose faith and dedication to the Lord refreshes my heart.

To my mentor and (spiritual) mother, Mamie: you planted spiritual truth in me and loved me like a mom. Thank you!

Thank you to my (adopted) mother, Patricia, who introduced me to the joys of prison ministry and continually encouraged me to write this book. Your constant affirmations inspired me to dare to believe this was possible. Thank you for all the editing you did on this project. I am so thankful that my birth mom willed me to you (her dear friend) upon her death.

To my ever-sweet (adopted) sister, Shirley: thank you for always believing in the call of God upon my life and for encouraging me all the way. Thank you for believing in this book so much that in spite of my procrastination, you flew me up to Alaska (all expenses paid) to get alone and begin writing.

To the most anointed editor, Shae Cooke: thank you for all the work you did on this project. I pray continually that God will bless you with a double portion for all you have done for me. You have been such a blessing and a very dear friend!

Thank you, Priscilla, at "Images 'N Photography," for the inspired headshots and photography. You are such a blessing to this ministry.

Thank you, Pastor Richard Heard and my family at Christian Tabernacle, for all your prayers and support during this project.

ENDORSEMENTS

First Corinthians 14:1 in the Living Bible says, *"Let love be your greatest aim...."* We are truly in a love war, and almost every day there are "love-tests" to pass. Ronda Brown in her book, *Healing Hidden Hurts,* gives tools, keys, and weapons that will minister healing to some of your deepest wounds—the ones that keep you from loving yourself and others. Her profound insights will help you become a warrior for love and to move forward in wholeness, rest, and strength. The truths revealed will remind you that...God loves you with an everlasting love. He really does!

Patricia King
Extreme Prophetic
www.XPmedia.com

One of the fastest ways to mature and grow in the supernatural realms of God is to be whole in Him. It takes a special courage to pursue that wholeness, but the days we currently live in are remarkably accelerated. Therefore, we have no time to waste and no time to live in regret. Ronda gives us key understanding in just how to move beyond ourselves, past the hurt, past the wounds, and step into a life of miraculous freedom. Join her in this journey and find your superhuman destiny!

Sharnael Wolverton
Swiftfire Ministries International
www.swiftfire.org

God has a wonderful plan for your life. If you have suffered hurts and unjustified wrongs that have left in their path bitter memories, woundedness, and fragmented pieces of your heart, then this book is for you. Often the memories of past scars keep us shackled to the pain and limit us in certain areas. *Healing Hidden Hurts* is sound biblical teaching with practical and easy techniques to finally be released from your past in order to advance into the wonderful destiny God has designed for you. If you have not been able to get the breakthrough yet that you desire, then this book is definitely for you. *Healing Hidden Hurts* will empower you to dare to believe that the fullness of healing can be yours.

Bill Henderson
Henderson International Ministries
www.WordOnTheStreet.com

CONTENTS

FOREWORD
by Stacey Campbell

As a prophet, the Lord gives me many words for people, most often for those whom I do not know and seldom (if ever) meet again. Imagine my delight when I heard from Ronda about how the word the Lord had me deliver to her about His restorative plans for her future had manifested in such a way that the "light and the new dawn" I prophesied had indeed profoundly arrived! My spirit danced! It thrills me to see God's hand in her life, to know how He has opened to this precious woman of God who has suffered so much an exceedingly abundant and exciting new future!

Healing Hidden Hurts is about tearing down the old mindset and breaking through to the new so that your history does *not* dictate your future. The restoration of God is available in every realm of your life, no matter how battered you are in body, mind, or spirit, or how far away you think God is.

Do you know why the book *The Shack* is so popular in the Church and in the secular marketplace? Because every one of us have hurts and need healing, and at one time or another have asked, "Where *are* You, God? …Don't You *see* what is happening to me?" That phenomenal best-seller gives hope to those who are hurting—those who feel that God does not care about them. *Healing Hidden Hurts* is a *true* story that deserves a place on the bookshelf alongside your copy of *The Shack*. Thousands, if not tens of hundreds of thousands, will relate to Ronda's heartbreak when she thought God was too far away to save her or rescue her children. Her experiences are *real,* and it is a journey that will also bring you to your knees rejoicing when you realize who you really are before God, how much He is aware of, and of His concern about your deepest pain, regrets, and issues of your heart.

Almost everyone in this world has been on the receiving end of someone's bad behavior—insults, injury, gossip, slander—and many are in a vicious cycle of victimization. Some, like Ronda, have suffered horrifically and repeatedly, *but* God offers good news to those hurt by sin: mercy, healing, and restoration from their woundedness, double honor for shame, and the grace and mercy to forgive their aggressor!

Hurting people hurt people. Ronda's journey and life are signs to the power of God that is available to us all. And this helps us avoid hurting ourselves and others and to forgive when it seems we have every right to hold on to an offense or even wreak our own vengeance.

No matter the trauma or heartbreak in your life—no matter where you are even in your walk with God—Ronda teaches how you can set yourself up for every blessing and turn negative events in your favor for a destiny and future more awesome than you could ever imagine possible. Learn how to stop that destructive cycle of victimization that pulls you away from God—or into believing that He doesn't care about you—cold in its tracks!

By His grace, and with the presence of His precious Holy Spirit accompanying her, Ronda revisits her past so that she can bring us all on a revelatory journey of love, of hope, of healing, of certainty in this day of uncertainty, and of faith in the reality of His tangible and very real love and presence, especially in our eleventh hours. I highly recommend *Healing Hidden Hurts* to anyone who needs a renewed sense of hope in this seesaw world in which we live.

If you're wondering where God is, pick up this book and read it; you'll find Him on *every* page.

Stacey Campbell
RevivalNOW! Ministries
www.RevivalNow.com

FOREWORD
by Dr. Richard Heard

As created beings, lovingly conceived in the mind of our heavenly Father, long before we were ever conceived in the womb of our earthly mothers, we were designed and fashioned to meet needs that exist in this fallen world. We were born with purpose, and without us, the earth and all of humanity are far less than what they could be.

Sometimes it's our achievements that inspire others and encourage them to greatness. Perhaps it's the music we write, the awards we earn, or the accomplishments of our lives that cause others to say they can do it too. At other times it's the struggles we survive and the difficulties we overcome, when in reality we shouldn't have made it, which bring hope to those who are themselves struggling and searching for far too elusive answers.

Nothing is more powerful than a testimony. With all of his degrees and great educational achievements, and with his powerful intellect and speaking abilities, Paul was still most effective when he told his personal testimony. On those occasions when he needed to persuade his audience, such as when he appeared before King Agrippa, Paul would tell his testimony rather than debate and argue theology! Why? Because a testimony is the story of a test that you might not have survived had it not been for God personally making a way where there had not been one before. It gives others hope that if God did it for you, then perhaps...just perhaps, He might do it for them too. And you know what? He will!

Ronda's testimony offers just this kind of hope. It is an incredible story of deliverance and restoration that will inspire and bless, as well as remind you that God is faithful and He loves you more than you could ever know. He has created you for greatness. And no matter what you are walking through, He is there with you and can deliver you, while restoring what the enemy thought he had taken from you for good.

Dr. Richard Heard
Senior Pastor: Christian Tabernacle
Houston, Texas

PROLOGUE

So great was the diabolical force on her that Ronda wanted out of this life. Seemingly in the devil's choke hold since before her birth, Ronda now felt that satan had her in a firm death grip. Assaulted from every side and suffering the greatest loss of her life, she walked the shores of last resort convinced that the best thing for her *was* death. Emotionally and physically battle-weary and drained of all resolve, she had nothing left of herself to fight with as the enemy waged a full-out frontal assault.

While still in her mother's womb, satan had tried to strangle her. As a child, fear and trauma had assailed her through the disappearance of her father: Missing in Action (MIA) war hero, SMAJ George Ron Brown (Vietnam/Laos 1968). As a teen, a spirit of rebellion had lured her into wrong choices and into a cruel, controlling, and abusive relationship—a perfect setup to have her lose hope, blame God, and even run from Him.

She had escaped, but fury fueled her adversary's resolve for revenge. The abuses and losses she had already suffered were nothing compared to the evil that would lurk and prey on Ronda and her two little girls in coming days.

The safety of escape was fleeting, but her Rescuer was on His way. The devil knew it and used terrorist tactics in a last-ditch effort to destroy her and her home. He pinned her down in his death grip on the precipice of the pit of hell.

This sandy shore of last resort, her personal Armageddon, would be the place of battles to save her and her children. Wrath, bitterness, blame, and unforgiveness sought to consume her; death infiltrated her thoughts. Satan raised his bloodied sword with the pain of the past and yesterday's regrets to destroy every shred of hope and faith she had left for a triumphant future.

But Passion appeared on the front lines with a heavenly host for backup in a supernatural display of signs, wonders, and miracles to dispel the myth and lie that the enemy had full reign over her life: past, present, and future.

Would Jesus...*could* Jesus restore the treasures of her life that rejection, fear, and despair had stolen? Could He take her from beginning to end to beginning again?

PART I

THE END

Chapter 1

Transforming Seasons

Unduly shamed and emotionally exhausted, I stood on the sandy beach staring out onto the horizon one warm June day in 1997…with plans to take my life. Life now existed for me only within the breath I breathed. This time, I was determined to do it, and the .38-caliber handgun in my bag was my insurance. I wanted to be free of the trauma, death, and destruction that spelled my life, and I no longer had breath left in me to fight the latest devastation. *How can I survive through this…how will I live without my children?*

My girls were the only things that mattered to me at all. So intertwined was my life and my very identity in them, that everything else was meaningless without their presence. Lies and false allegations in court had called into question my ability to parent and protect them adequately. My ex-husband had seemed to gleam with pride under oath as he made false accusations of misconduct and physical abuse—the tools he would use to punish me for divorcing him. Removing the children from my custody had just been an added benefit for him. Unfortunately, hurting people hurt other people, just as healing people heal other people. As time went on, the hurt was evident, and I was the target, no matter that the children would be hurt most in this process.

For the past ten months...*ten months!*...I had only been allowed to visit Lillian and Lacie[1] under court-supervised visitation. *Oh, what I would give to hold them again!* I wasn't even allowed to *hug* my little ones. Though the allegations were unsubstantiated, the courts informed me that I was permanently losing *all* parental rights. Sometimes things that happen to us can seem so unfair, but God has a plan even though we can't always see it at the moment. Sometimes it can be to build our character, strengthen us, or make our faith stronger.

DISAPPOINTMENT WITH GOD

In times past, this ocean spot had always been a place of enjoyment where my girls and I often played along the water's edge. Alone on the now-deserted shore, I had resolved that this would be my last walk along this path of bittersweet memories. Freedom from a lifetime of being a victim of misfortune was just a trigger-pull away.

All I could see in my mind's eye were the empty, devastating pages of what had been my existence. Pain, rejection, abuse—a lifetime of struggles. I felt disappointed and rejected by man and God. Why did I always feel so powerless when it came to improving the quality of my life? Where was God in my hurt, in my struggles?

Time for reflection was over. The only option I could see was to end the miserable existence that imprisoned me. I had tried to break through, I truly had, but death now seemed the only escape.

The calming sound of the waves lapping along the shore did little to distract my attention away from the closure I desperately sought.

A Death Target

The enemy had targeted me before I was born and had tried to take me out before I even took my first breath. A stray dog attacked and bit my mother while she made her way to the hospital in labor with me. Though she suffered only a single dog bite the trauma she endured set the stage for my difficult delivery. During the actual labor and delivery, the umbilical cord knotted as a noose around my neck. Each contraction stopped my heart and brought me one heartbeat closer to death.

At two years old, a piece of Thanksgiving stuffing lodged in my throat. Choking to death, I was blue when my father, a trained paramedic, administered CPR.

Death, rejection, abuse, abandonment, and fear assailed my mother early on in her life too. On the very night of her ninth birthday, her mother died at home from ovarian cancer. Her father's alcoholism worsened, and his abuse and rejection of my mother intensified her personal pain. So began her cycle of dysfunction and insecurity, pain and fear, as he abandoned her to his own desires. My birth was a ray of light to her. Although I was conceived out of wedlock, she and my father were anxious for my arrival, and quickly married. For a short time, we were a happy and functional young family.

MISSING IN ACTION

However, it was 1968, and the Vietnam War was in full force when rejection established its foothold in my life. A black sedan drove up to our modest home, and its occupants handed my mother a letter: "The Army regrets to inform you that Sgt. Major Brown is Missing in Action...." SMAJ George Ron Brown was my father. He had been in Laos running special operations with the Special Forces. The complicated words in this letter brought my little world crashing down.

Missing in action...MIA. I was only 6 and did not even truly understand what it meant. Of course he would come home! He was not dead! My dad would return. We held out hope, though with each passing day the void of abandonment grew in our hearts.

I remember like yesterday...sitting glued to our television for hours reading every name and studying each face as the prisoner-of-war victims, one by one, appeared unannounced from rescue planes at the close of the Vietnam War. *The next man could be my father,* I thought, only to go to bed that night as devastated as the day we first received the news.

Each year the government made us unfulfilled new promises of hope and recovery. In the end, we never received news beyond what they told us that initial day. Today his heroic name is all we have of him, and it quietly rests on a black marble monument known as "The Wall" in Washington D.C. (on Panel 46E-Line 53).

GRIEF, BLAME, AND REBELLION

The days turned to years, and I cannot remember a time that was not filled with sadness and crying. The words of Psalm 56:8 were not a comfort to me—I could not understand—*"You number my wanderings;* [and] *put my tears into Your bottle"* (NKJV). Yet a youngster, depression plagued me—the grief was more than I could bear. Death's closure was a luxury I was never given; therefore, I'd pine and mourn day after day over a loss that I couldn't call "death." Grief turned to blame. I blamed God for destroying my world and for taking what I secretly felt was the "wrong parent" from me.

My father's disappearance wreaked havoc on my mother as she tried with all her might to hold on to what little she felt she had left. That would be me. At least I felt that by the way she treated me. My mother dealt with her personal grief through extreme manipulation and control, often lashing out at me. As a victim of her verbal and emotional abuse, I increasingly felt devoid of any emotions other than sorrow and loss. The harder she came against me, the faster I ran, especially as I entered into my young teen years. Her constant boyfriends paraded in and out of my unstable world, and confused hurt brought its own form of abuse.

As a result, rebellion fueled my search for love, but I found it in "all the wrong places," as the cliché goes. By my senior year in high school, I was out of control. I would have done anything to escape my home, the pain, the extreme control, and the miserable memories. Consequently, I gravitated toward older men who could fulfill the desperate need I had for a father's love. In 1980, I met a man 14 years my senior, and we were married immediately after my senior high school graduation—after only a few weeks of courtship and much to my mother's disapproval. He was quick to "love" me. Because of all the pain that I endured, I was very vulnerable and easily persuaded to be in a relationship that would turn out to be extremely dysfunctional and abusive. He appeared successful, accomplished, mature, and financially stable, so it wasn't so hard for me to overlook concerns I had about his complex personality.

I desperately desired to be loved. In hindsight, my thinking was that I was lucky that anyone could want me, so I had better take advantage of his quick offer of marriage. *This might be my only chance to have a family*, I thought. The dream of finally being loved and of raising my own child, the hope of fulfilling the longing for children of my own, superseded the red flags waving in my heart about his character.

With plans that I thought were near perfect, I determined to prove to my family that they were wrong about him, and that someone could love me and provide stability in my life. So I forged ahead, determined to fulfill what I felt was my primary purpose and calling: to be the best mother I could be despite my mother's conditional and abusive example.

SALVATION AND CHURCH

When I was a child, my family and I had attended an Episcopal church—but we had little knowledge of Jesus. When I was in my mid-teens, my mom had a salvation experience that began to change our spiritual direction. We then transferred to a non-denominational church and attended more frequently. Though initially our family unit *appeared* healthy and strong, dysfunction always brewed just under the surface. Lonely, confused, angry, and rebellious throughout most of my teen years, I attended church only to appease mom. Nothing I attempted brought about lasting peace. However, I can now recall, even through my rebellion, that God always kept His hand on me, frequently giving me cryptic dreams about a ministry with Him.

I was tired of running from what I knew to be right and frustrated with seemingly always making the wrong decisions. I desperately desired even a shred of stability and happiness in my life.

Shortly before my marriage to Jerry, I made the personal choice to walk to the altar one Sunday morning and dedicate my heart to Jesus. Though there were no big bells, whistles, or earth-moving experiences, my troubled heart started to feel some peace for the first time.

Jerry and I actually met at church. After service one day I met Jerry, and he asked me out for ice cream. After a short courtship, we married—just two short months later.

Following my marriage to Jerry, I began pursuing a life pleasing to the Father through the pathway of purity and holiness. I trusted God to change Jerry's heart, praying to Him that Jerry (who also boasted of being a born-again Christian) could love me, believing that he would learn to love as he witnessed my love for him through Jesus. Even from the outset, my marriage to Jerry was turbulent. While driving to the church to exchange vows, I suspected I was making a mistake, but being as headstrong as I was, I figured I could still make it work out, and my own pride prevented me from admitting that maybe I was wrong. Within a few months of marriage, I knew I had made a rash decision and a grave mistake, but the alternative meant returning back home to a life I fought so hard to break free of. Once married, I discovered Jerry had an addiction to prescription drugs and alcohol that controlled who he was. At the time, I felt I had no choice but to submit and comply with his abusive nature. I continually lived in fear for myself.

Throughout, Jerry and I always attended church together—but that did not help our relationship at all. His lack of relationship and commitment to God prevented us from having peace in our lives.

Desiring to conceive a child as soon as we were married, I begged him for children. But he threatened to end our marriage if I brought a child into his life before he was ready. Every year I cried to begin a family. My heart's desire was to have a large family—a house full of children.

The Joy of Parenthood

After years of my impatient waiting, he relented, "allowing" me to conceive. *At last!* It was all I thought about! Immediately I conceived, and in 1984, our first daughter, Lillian, was born.

Years of daydreaming about how I could improve my child's quality of life began to materialize for me. I had so many plans, hopes, dreams, and desires to enrich her life.

Yes, I wanted more children—more joy—and constantly begged Jerry, "Please?" But he forbade me. "I can only love one child," he said, even though Lillian kept praying to the Lord at every mealtime and bedtime for a sister. She pled and pled until one day I confronted Jerry again, "Please…this is pitiful. Can we try?" I so looked forward to pregnancy—each phase thrilled me. I could make it a career; I loved it so much. My three-hour natural delivery was a breeze!

My husband relented, but his reluctance—and perhaps his own childhood nightmares—surfaced well into my pregnancy. "You had better not produce a boy—I can never love a male child…" he threatened.

Fraught with fear now of what he might do should our child be a boy, I prayed daily for God's mercy. *"Please—let me have a girl."*

God answered, with Lacie, another beautiful and perfect daughter in 1988. Lillian, rightfully believing that God had specifically answered her prayers for a new baby, claimed the infant as her very own! Often I would get up in the night to check on Lacie only to find out that her now-five-year-old sister had removed her from her crib and taken her to her own bed.

They were so inseparable that during our divorce proceedings the psychologist—whom Jerry had hired to prove me a crazy and unfit mother—testified in court that in the history of his career, our two daughters were the closest siblings he'd ever come across and that in "*no way* should these best friends be separated."

My beautiful angels were truly a gift from God to teach me a love I had never known. Theirs was an example to me of the Father's perfect and unconditional love. In turn, I was able to understand what unconditional love *toward* God meant.

Through many various lessons, I experienced depths of healing from my dysfunctional childhood that brought new joy as I found creative ways even to express my love to the children. We routinely enjoyed long nature walks through the parks and fields behind our home. There was little time for television as we explored the many wonders of nature outdoors and the marvels of history at the many museums we visited. We would plan our weekly expeditions with delighted expectancy. Every day seemed an adventure in learning, and our knowledge grew together as we visited long-forgotten ghost towns, native dwellings, gold mines, and historical sites. Often we would do crafts from our adventures following our outings, reinforcing what we learned.

We were rock hounds, too, collecting interesting stones from each place. The girls even transformed their outdoor playhouse into a working rock museum, charging the neighborhood children a quarter to view the hundreds of rock and fossil specimens, which they had painstakingly and carefully collected, categorized, and labeled.

Industrious were my two girls! They even mass-produced their crafts and sold them door-to-door in their loaded red wagon. Neighbors succumbed to their charm, as each sale provided the bonus of a complimentary song and dance—

scores they wrote and choreographed themselves.

Reading was a passion, and the local library was just down the street. It was not long before the girls converted the rock museum to a personal lending library of previously discarded books they had collected at yard and garage sales. Lillian developed an elaborate record system that categorized the over 400 books in their collection! They charged an entrance fee that included the loan/free checkout of a book. Business was good for my girls: profit margins were high, and they were developing stellar office, sales, and marketing skills!

For two years I home-schooled the girls, and life itself became our classroom. Walks on the beach evolved into lessons of science, creation, and math as they learned about creation and God's order of things; they learned how to identify many different items and understand their purposes. Learning was an adventure, and they excelled such that when they did enter Christian private school, Lillian tested years above the other children in most areas.

Some might say that I over-devoted my time to the girls, that there wasn't balance. Nevertheless, I felt I was doing my life's work—they, in my heart, were my destiny and divine purpose, and they surely would not have to suffer the rejection, heartbreak, conditional love, abuse, and control that I had lived in as a child.

Jerry did not seem to mind or care about the time I spent with the girls because he was wrapped up in his own world, building his financial empire and pursuing his interest in law enforcement which consumed his time. In fact, he would brag sometimes to his friends about how I home-schooled them. However, he later turned it around in court, claiming that I purposely over-sheltered the girls as a means of controlling them.

CONTROL AND ABUSE

Jerry rarely joined us on our adventurous excursions or involved himself with home routines. His schedule kept him busy. What with running his insurance company by day and volunteering his time at night in law enforcement, there wasn't much time for home. He often stopped by the house to check up on us while on patrol, but other than that, his life did not interact much with ours.

For that I thank the Lord, because Jerry was a classic textbook abuser. His anger escalated in the evenings after they had gone to bed. I could endure his controlling, abusive nature as long as the children were not the brunt of it, as long as they did not find out, and as long as it happened after they were asleep. I did not want the children to find out or to upset the family balance. In my view, they needed a father. They would not grow up without a father in their lives, as I did. When they awoke in the morning, I greeted them cheerfully—they would never suspect my secret painful reality, the bruises I always managed to explain away. No one suspected my personal hell.

This was not martyrdom for the sake of my children. Understand that I had nowhere else to go, no money, and no one willing to help. Jerry demanded that I have no contact with my mother or sister. When Mom moved out of state, we lost contact altogether because he did not allow me to call or even write. Years later, my mother confessed that he had contacted her to fill her head with untruths and lies, telling her that I hated her and warning her to stay away from me. For the last eight years of my marriage, I did not see any family.

Powerless—I felt helpless to leave. Later, hopelessness and fear set in especially when Jerry routinely threatened that if I ever left him, he would hunt me down and kill me, or ensure the children were taken away from me, or both. Who was I to disbelieve him in light of his extremely volatile and violent temperament and the fact that he was already in law enforcement and bragged about the ability to use his status to hurt me and spread doubt and slander about me?

Jerry made excellent money as a financial planner, selling life insurance, investments, retirement plans, and trust accounts. Jerry completely controlled our finances. I never knew how much was in the bank account. A small allowance for groceries, housing incidentals, and limited personal needs was all I received. Often my allowance was not enough to meet our bills, and I would suffer through fits of his rage as punishment. Every financial record he had he kept locked in a special briefcase that always went with him.

His abuse escalated to such a degree that I feared the turning of the key in the lock of the front door; my stomach knotted with fear as I anticipated the worst. I didn't know what my husband would conjure up from day-to-day as he delighted in finding new ways to torment me. He would often instigate a fight just so that he'd have an excuse to leave the house again to go out on patrol.

To outsiders—we appeared normal. Few suspected that I had lived for years with such hardship. Jerry was 100 percent more controlling than my mother ever was. Everything with him was a battle, and with each clash, a part of me numbed and died. There was physical abuse on top of his ridiculing tongue; my emotions seesawed constantly by his emotionally battering words. With the constant stress and fear, my hair would fall out; I suffered daily nosebleeds and had extreme digestive problems. A chiropractor friend treated me for free for years because I needed spinal adjustments several times a week for the chronic pain that this unending stress brought on.

Little by little my husband's complexities, his mysterious lapses in time, his concealed secret life outside of the home, the lack of accountability regarding our finances, and the silent alarms I had heard and ignored at the outset of our short courtship resounded loudly. His addiction to prescription drugs, I would later find out, had been a problem as well in previous relationships. I would discover later that he had been married several times before and had children as well.

During my divorce, I was able to track down two of those wives. They reported that he had so traumatized them that they did not want their location revealed, with one even changing her name and leaving the state to avoid his vengeance.

JERRY'S BACKGROUND

Over the span of many years I was able to piece together a tremendous amount of information about Jerry and his past. Here is what I learned:

Jerry's background wasn't pretty. At 16, he was heavily involved with Mexican gangs and was arrested for drug trafficking and felony auto theft. Authorities gave him two choices: jail time or the military. He chose the latter and completed four years, which included one tour in Vietnam, where he sustained a wound that required a transfusion of blood. They sent him to a Japanese hospital to recover. Just prior to entering the military, he married his first wife and had a son. She filed for divorce during the time he was stationed in Japan. She took their son and never allowed Jerry to see him. They had no contact after their divorce.

Following his stint in the military, Jerry returned to Okinawa and there met and married his second wife with whom he had a daughter. Jerry opened a nightclub adjacent to the military base. The club was a cover for drug dealing. His customers were military personnel and village locals. Japanese police raided the establishment, arrested Jerry for heroin trafficking, and sentenced him to three-and-a-half years in a civilian, maximum-security prison in Japan. Almost immediately after he served his sentence, he returned to America, but not before he was able to take his daughter and bring her back to the States with him. His motive for keeping the child separated from her mother was only to cause pain to the mother for ending their relationship during his incarceration. I only learned of the relationship because she began calling our home after we were married begging to see her child. A local Japanese woman, she had relocated to the States for the sole purpose of finding and being a part of her daughter's life. Jerry never allowed the mother to see or talk to her daughter or to have any knowledge of the child. She was never permitted to be a part of her daughter's life until the child was much older and began a search for her mother. He had no interest in his children and left his daughter with anyone who would take her—neighbors, his sister, and his "so-called" friends.

When I met him at the church, his third relationship had just dissolved, and with her, he'd had another daughter. The mother had taken the child and run from Jerry, preventing him from being a part of the child's life.

DISEASE STRIKES

It is unclear if Jerry caught hepatitis C from his IV, heroin drug use, or from the blood transfusion due to his military wound, but during my pregnancy with Lacie around 1988, he began to show signs of severe liver damage and reoccurring bouts of hepatitis. After a long and difficult battle for his life, in May of 1992 he received a liver transplant. Recovery was slow and extremely trying on me and the children, then only ages 8 and 4. The transplant team had a difficult time keeping the liver healthy, and he suffered 12 separate organ rejections in the course of a year. The only treatment at the time was Prednisone, a steroid that augmented his aggression. After the 12th rejection, the doctors informed us that he was going to need a second transplant.

"Lord, heal him, or take him home," I prayed silently. How all of us could get through another year of this…I did not know. The first surgery and his recovery, his increased aggression, not to mention the financial burden—it all seemed too much to bear. He was physically sick and became frustrated emotionally. In the months to come, his anger continued to escalate.

ENDNOTE

1. Names have been changed to protect their privacy.

CHAPTER 2

FIRE BY DAY, TERROR BY NIGHT

Even in his weakened state, Jerry controlled us, providing few financial resources for even our most basic needs. The girls needed new clothes badly, and so did I. I scrounged for discount remnant fabrics and sewed clothes using the same pattern repeatedly. I recall the church offering me some clothes donated by the family of an elderly woman who had passed on to be with the Lord. It was an answer to my prayers, and I was so thankful to God for that donation.

If only I could make some extra money, the girls and I would be OK. I recalled hearing an interview on a Christian radio talk show some time prior to Jerry's transplant about a woman who asked God for just one business idea to help her bring in additional finances. She said that the Lord had answered her prayers. He gave her an idea, and her business netted her massive amounts of income. Well, I just loved the concept of asking God for a creative business idea. Understanding that God is no respecter of persons, I asked Him night after night for several months in 1993 for a business idea that would help the girls and me along financially.

DIVINE INSPIRATION

One evening during my prayer time, I specifically heard the Lord tell me, "Get Jerry on herbs." Jerry was much sicker now and awaiting the second transplant. I barely understood how to season spaghetti—let alone use herbal medicine to develop a form of treatment for specific ailments—but I knew I had heard the Lord correctly. Over a period of several weeks in the early part of 1994, the Lord continued to remind me to get Jerry on herbs, but I didn't know where to turn—and had no knowledge of the medicinal properties of herbs.

Visits to health food stores yielded few results. How was I to fulfill God's directive if I could not discover anything? Nothing I could find was specifically formulated to target organs or specific areas—just general formulas for overall health and well-being. Frustrated, I returned home without the supplements I knew he needed.

But my disappointment was short-lived. On one of my weekly visits to the library with the girls, the strangest thing happened! Normally we entered through the door closest to the children's book section and bee-lined straight for their books. However on this particular day, for some reason, we took a different route that required us to go past the adult section. On the way through I tripped over something and fell on my face—literally—nose on carpet! I picked up the offending obstacle: a book. Title? *Herbal Medicine.* I just about fell on the floor again! How great is our God? I hadn't even known to look for such a book, and suddenly there it was! Henceforth, I read every book the library had on herbs, and miraculously the Lord empowered me supernaturally to commit everything I learned to memory.

A few months after I had originally heard the Lord tell me to get Jerry on herbs, I was again up in the wee hours and praying. The presence of the Lord came to me, downloading into my mind a series of herbal formulas for Jerry's use. The Lord told me exactly which herbs to blend and precisely how many milligrams of each were required. Birthed literally from the throne of God Himself, I held in my hands four specific organ-rebuilding formulas: a liver cleanser, kidney cleanser, colon cleanser, and blood purifier. To my knowledge, these were the first of their kind that targeted specific organs. The Lord told me exactly how to grind the herbs using a small coffee grinder, and how to pack them into gelatin capsules. Then He instructed me to drive about one hour south to the city where I would find a small Chinese tea store that would supply bulk herbs, which I did.

I made up the formulas exactly as God showed me, gave them to my bedridden husband, and waited. The results were amazing. Within four months, Jerry no longer needed the second transplant. His blood work, SGOT, and SGPT (liver enzymes) returned to normal as did his Gamma GT, and before long he was able to return to work and to patrol. Even his follow-up transplant specialists were amazed by the miraculous results of his recovery. One doctor confided that he secretly suffered from hepatitis C himself and asked for my herbal formulations.

News traveled fast, and people we knew called requesting the same formulas that Jerry had been on. With their successes, they spread the information even more. Before long, people all over the country were calling me—people I had never met—asking for these "miracle formulas." How they got my telephone number I will never know, but their many dramatic healing results and testimonies constantly amazed me.

I was in business before I even realized I was, making up herb capsules in my kitchen until the early hours of the morning. Jerry wasn't too pleased at first. He didn't like the fact that I was gaining recognition and likely felt that I was slipping out of his control. It was a fight to accomplish what I did. We were both a little concerned as well about potential lawsuits against our kitchen business. I knew that if things were to progress, I'd have to provide a high quality product professionally manufactured, bottled, and labeled.

I begged Jerry to help the business financially, and by and by, he knew a good thing when he saw it. However, instead of *giving* me the money (as perhaps a husband should have), he only agreed to *"float me a loan"* of $2,000, which I was to pay back as soon as possible, even though this was a family business.

With that money I was able to get the formulas professionally manufactured, bottled, and labeled. Health food market chains heard about my story, requested my formulas, and by the end of 1994, I was in business full time—a divine business! Because of a prayer for one business idea and God answering my plea to help my sick husband, I was thrust into the marketplace almost overnight. With no business training or understanding at the outset, I learned daily and step-by-step, but I credit it completely to divine wisdom from the Lord.

Jerry improved and grew stronger every day with the herbs and anti-rejection medication, but so did his rage which fueled the control he thrived on. As my business quickly expanded and my income increased, so did his violence, especially now that he felt powerless to stop me. He'd forbid me to negotiate large deals or even attend key meetings that would have greatly expanded my company. Jealousy fueled his fury, especially as the business grew. Prominent businesses representing the health community asked me to speak or grant an interview. I was even invited to co-host a live health talk show on Saturdays, and that blossomed into other invitations to give radio interviews with key health promoters whose syndication spanned four Midwest states.

One of my clients, a doctor, contacted me with a lead. He knew the buyer (his family member) of a well-known corporation whose headquarters was looking for a line of herbal products for their vast chain of stores. He guaranteed that he would successfully bring my herbal products to the forefront in exchange for a commission, which I was glad to pay.

Everything was set. The meeting date with the buyers and all the preparations were made, but Jerry forbade me to go, threatening me not to proceed. He did everything in his power to successfully shut down all negotiations. Sadly, as a result the corporation went with a different line.

ADVICE AND COUNSELING

With Jerry better now—the abuse escalated. By 1995 I desperately wanted out of the marriage and sought the counsel of a minister. He told me that if I divorced my husband, I would "burn in hell," and that there was "no forgiveness for divorce." I stayed for another agonizing year, believing in what was actually incorrect and ungodly advice and praying for life to spring forth in our dead marriage.

During this time, I saw several Christian and secular therapists, and while I experienced amazing personal and spiritual growth, my marriage still struggled. I pled with Jerry to work on the relationship, begged him to attend Christian marriage counseling with me. He agreed and attended only two sessions but refused to participate unless he could point a finger at me. "Our problems are all her fault!" he'd scream, describing my faults and his faultlessness. He refused to take any responsibility for the deterioration of our marriage. At the last session, the therapist stood, closed her file, and asked him to leave. She said that if his attitude was to continue in that hateful and uncooperative manner there was little she could do to help us.

At my personal one-on-one follow-up meeting later that week, she said that the marriage was likely doomed for failure as he was "unwilling to even admit any fault and lacked the desire to try or work on any issue."

I KNEW THERE WAS A BETTER WAY OF LIFE, BUT IT DID NOT SEEM TO EXIST FOR ME.

I knew there was a better way of life, but it did not seem to exist for me. Jerry operated through total control and fear tactics and tried to scare me into doing what he wanted me to do. For example, throughout our marriage he would routinely leave graphic, gruesome rape and crime scene photographs on the counter for the girls and me to see and routinely told us, "This is what happens to women who go out at night."

The more emotionally healthy I grew, the worse Jerry got. Sometimes he would confide, "I'm losing control, and I don't know how to regain it." Those fears manifested in violence, and by the end of our 16th year of marriage, I feared for my very life and the safety of our girls.

EVIL RAMPAGE

Toward the final year of our marriage, I seriously contemplated divorce and gained the courage to locate my mother and sister and restore a relationship with them. One weekend my mother was ill, and I took the girls to see her for the weekend. This infuriated Jerry, and he went on a dangerous rampage of violence and destruction. In his mind, he could force us to stay with him if I had no money and no means to earn a living. I never really knew why he would not let go of me.

We returned from the weekend to carnage. Most of my personal belongings he destroyed, tore up, or disposed of: letters and cards from my deceased father and grandmother, clothes, books, everything he could get his hands on. Neighbors admitted that they witnessed Jerry take more than five 30-gallon trash bags of my personal items out of the house that weekend to the dumpsters.

But the damage didn't end there. He hit the offices I leased for my thriving business. Jerry destroyed my computers and other valuables. He arranged for my 800 phone number to be cut off to prevent client contact and then removed and permanently destroyed my inventory—hundreds of bottles of each herbal formula. He wiped out my client database and files, removed all of my marketing material, and went to the bank and withdrew every penny from my business checking account. As quickly as my business had begun, it was over, and I was financially destitute again.

For added insurance, he bragged that he'd had our home wired with bugging devices so he'd know my every move. Then he sabotaged my car in the garage and slashed the tires so I wouldn't dare leave again.

Things grew much worse as he exercised almost deadly force in his madness to control my every move. In the middle of 1995 he'd restrain me upstairs and threaten me if I tried to go downstairs. He especially enjoyed torturing me in the night while I slept by jumping on me, pinning me beneath his weight, and strangling me to the point just before I passed out. Sometimes he'd wake me by threateningly slapping his police baton into his hand just inches above my face.

So that I couldn't call for help, he jerked phone wires from the walls. One night he removed the bullets from his gun without me knowing. Then he pushed me into a corner, held the gun inches from my face, and pulled the trigger. I thought I would die in that instant. It was horrifying.

Throughout the marriage, he often shoved me against a wall with a hand around my throat while he punched his fist into the wall, inches from my face. Twice he hid our daughters from me—sent them to his police friends—in an effort to get me to comply with his wishes.

My terror mounted, especially when one of his police friends actually called me to "warn" that they had overheard his plans to place a bomb under my car and that he mentioned that he wanted to put a contract "hit" out on my life. Even though we lived in a small town, my contact with his co-workers was very minimal.

I could see Jerry's fury growing toward the girls as well, and it seemed like it was only a matter of time before he would really hurt them too.

Many people would later ask me why I did not end the marriage sooner. At the time I felt there were several reasons to persevere: fear of losing my children, my desperate desire to provide a father for my children, and the constant hope that each new day would bring salvation and deliverance from the Father to my husband. All those things bound me to a situation that I did not know how to escape.

FURY UNLEASHED

It was Saturday morning. Jerry was sleeping in, as he had gotten home late from patrol. The girls (now ages 7 and 11) and I were playing with the family dog downstairs. Our laughter resounded throughout the house and accidentally woke Jerry. He came down to investigate and saw the fun-play. At first, we thought he wanted to participate as he jokingly joined in on the chase. Then without incident or warning, he grabbed a belt, pulled down Lillian's pants, threw her to the ground cornering her against the wall, and beat her repeatedly until she could hardly stand.

Screaming, "Stop!" I grabbed him. I tried to stop him but he would not stop. He kept pushing me away as he continued to beat her little body. Then he released his full fury and pent-up rage upon her as she lay curled in the fetal position, helpless, and crying on the floor.

When it was over, I helped her upstairs and washed her badly beaten, swollen, and welted back and buttocks. Never before had I witnessed such unprovoked violence against a child. I was horrified. Yet even as we climbed those steps, he threatened me not to report it because "the county would remove both girls," and I would lose them.

During the week, Lacie also reported to me that Jerry told them that I had tried to abort my pregnancies and had never wanted them. In an attempt to pit one child against the other and against me, he said that if we divorced, I would put them up for adoption because I never really loved them. Another time he lied to the girls, said I was having an affair, and warned them not to kiss or touch me because he knew that I was dying of AIDS. Then he purposely instructed them on how to rebel against me and, if need be, to run away from home.

THE LAST STRAW

All his lies to the girls and the beating of Lillian were the last straw. Finally, I determined that "burning in hell" would be a better choice than remaining in that loveless and wildly dangerous marriage. I snuck out of the house and went directly to the court for a restraining order, one of many I would get against him. However, because of his law enforcement connections, every order I received mysteriously disappeared from court files.

As our divorce heated up, the lines were being drawn. In one of our last conversations, Jerry vowed, "If you continue with this crazy divorce, I will do everything in my power to destroy you emotionally, physically, and financially." As he made that unrighteous vow his life's ambition, he threatened that he was about to embark upon a master plan that would forever destroy me if I didn't take him back.

It turns out that I underestimated his intentions and ability. Had I known what would ensue in coming days, weeks, months, and even years, I doubt that I would have had the courage to leave.

His crazy, demonic antics grew even more dangerous when he repeatedly tried to run my car off the road, often with our children in the back seat. He would follow my car and harass me no matter where I went. Neighbors saw him sitting in the bushes around my home with binoculars and a loaded shotgun, and they called the police. But the police reports mysteriously disappeared, "lost," no doubt because of Jerry's "status" as Reserve Police Lieutenant.

There was a glimmer of light, however, when a detective in a neighboring county somehow came across our file and actively attempted to have Jerry charged with stalking. The detective arranged meetings with the District Attorney. As a result, I met with the District Attorney on several occasions as the case was built, but just before it was to go to trial, the charges were mysteriously dropped and nothing more was said about it.

However, just before our divorce was final, he was successful in having Jerry terminated from the police department. Jerry contested, pleading that he wanted to resign on record, and it was granted. He never worked in law enforcement again.

CHAPTER 3

THE ACCUSER

As Jerry's master plan unfolded, the skillfully planned details were more horrifying than I could have imagined. Never in my wildest dreams could I have dreamed up what he did next.

He reported to Child Protective Services (CPS) with fabricated, graphic, disgusting details in February 1996 that I was abusing my girls. Among many other things, he claimed that I routinely hooked the children up to an electrical device that would administer a painful electrical jolt as a means of disciplining them for lying.

INITIAL INVESTIGATIVE REPORT FROM CPS

The social worker's first investigation failed to substantiate Jerry's allegations and, in fact, raised alarm about Jerry to CPS.

The report is below. Usually such information is considered classified, but it was accidentally faxed to my attorney, and subsequently given to me.

Department of Social Services
Children's Services Bureau
To: Family Court Services[1]

1996

As we discussed over the phone this morning, I continue to have grave concerns about the well-being of the children [ages 8 & 12] of Ronda and Jerry XXXX. I have been unable to substantiate allegations that the mother abused the children, though I did find inappropriate boundaries being exercised by the father, especially with the youngest daughter, Lacie.

I have interviewed the children three times, the mother several times, and the father at least three times (counting phone contacts with dad and mom). The girls have told me that they fear for their mother's safety because of the father's extreme animosity towards Ronda. In addition, Lacie has told me that she covers up for Lillian—"takes the blame when her sister has done something because she knows her dad will not punish her, whereas Lillian would be in 'major trouble.'"

The father has accused the mother (in front of the minors) of being "a pathological liar…an adulterous whore…a woman doomed to burn in Hell," etc.

He promised me, in our last initial face-to-face interview, that he would no longer make derogatory remarks about his ex-wife in front of his children; per the children, he continues to "bad-mouth" her constantly and rave about her many alleged sins.

Father has stated to me that the mother is one hundred percent responsible for all their problems. She has lied about everything, and he himself is completely blameless. He has accused me of being biased toward the mother, who he claims is an accomplished liar and who can fool almost anybody. He has unequivocally denied ever hitting the mother except by accident. He says he has never harassed or threatened her. The girls both say this is not true, that he has hit mom on numerous occasions.

Lacie is far more likely to say, "I don't know" when her response would normally be negative for dad. However, she has witnessed one incident in a grocery store, which showed her that her father lied about something important (which concept totally floored her, since dad was always accusing mom of being the liar). She has now done an about-face, declaring that she does not want to visit her father, whom she previously had wanted to see as much as possible.

The girls, both who had been eagerly anticipating the beginning of [private] school, were removed from the school, related to the mother by the school principal, who notified her that Jerry had said he wouldn't support the girls in school. The father told me that the principal himself had removed the girls, "because he didn't want anything to do with anybody as crazy as Ronda, who told him horrible untrue things about me."

Jerry said he had gone in to pay his half of their school bills and been told by the principal that Ronda had not paid a cent. He reiterated that the principal—not he himself—had been responsible for removing the girls from school. Jerry insisted that I call the principal to confirm his story to show me what a liar and unfit mother his ex-wife is. I spoke directly with the principal who stated that Jerry had contacted him a second time to get him to say that the principal had insisted on the removal not Jerry. The principal told Jerry that was a lie, that Jerry had been the one to say he "would not support the girls in this school." Jerry kept saying to the principal that this was all a matter of miscommunication.

The principal told me that he wants to keep the girls in the school but only if Ronda has full custody because he is afraid of what Jerry will do if he has a legal reason to be on their campus. "I have witnessed first hand how volatile he is, and I am afraid for our school. I am also very much afraid for Ronda and the girls." He indicated that he thinks the father is unbalanced and extremely dangerous.

Jerry violated a restraining order when he brought the girls home to their mom and insisted on coming into the house to pick up some items. When I questioned him about this, he said his attorney had insisted that he go into the home, that he and Ronda had to communicate for the sake of the girls. I asked why they had not exchanged the girls at a neutral spot, as is usual when there is so much animosity between parties. Again he said his attorney had ordered this, despite the fact that a restraining order was in effect.

Ronda states that she hired a company, which found that her phone was tapped. Jerry had said this was all part of her paranoia. As to the bruises she had from Saturday's altercation in her home, Jerry insists she must have inflicted this herself when the police left her alone in the home for a minute. He says she attacked him by hitting him on the back of the neck; he turned around and may have shoved her off balance by accident as they were on the stairs in her home. When I told him that the youngest daughter said dad hit mom on accident, he said, "That's just Ronda putting words into their mouths! Give them to me for a week and see if they don't do a 180-degree turn." I reminded him that he had had them for eleven days previously and that the girls had only been back with her briefly: "It would only take her an hour to get them to say whatever she wants," he replied.

He told the police that Ronda had attacked him first and that he had been merely defending himself. He denied that he had rubbed at his neck (as Lillian says she witnessed him from her bedroom window) to increase the redness. He then suggested that Ronda, whom he claims not to have hit, must have caused her own bruises. When I queried the disparity between their physical abilities to protect themselves, he said, "Oh, a black belt can't get hurt?" He claims she is a violent woman. The only proof I have of this statement is his word, as the girls have told me this is not true, though she does try to defend herself and the girls.

I took this case to consult this morning shortly after talking with you. The committee shared my concerns about the girls (both physically and emotionally) but felt this is a matter for Family Court rather than CPS. The father has not hurt the girls, though he has inflicted injuries on the mother (which he denies). The mother says there have been prior instances in the past when marks were left by the father but that he told her (and she believed him, as he has been a volunteer reserve police officer for 13 plus years) that if she made a report, CPS would immediately come and take the girls away from both parents.

Lacie is now admitting that she has, contrary to court orders, been sleeping in the bed with her father over their last visit. As stated previously, Lacie now feels betrayed and manipulated by her father. She is very angry about this.

I feel very strongly that Jerry is a man in the throes of extreme danger and that he is probably a danger to himself and definitely a threat to his ex-wife and his daughters. He has access to guns and knives, and he is trained to use both. He has threatened, "That if he cannot have the girls, no one will." He told me he would prefer they were in foster care to living in the home with "their unfit mother." They expressed to me their concern that he might keep them or disappear with them if he were to get the chance.

Though Jerry may not hurt his daughters physically, the emotional damage being currently done to them is incalculable. I do not believe this damage is coming from the mother, as he continues to insist, accepting not a single bit of blame for their current situation.

I do not want to take the girls into protective custody as I feel they should not be separated from their mother. However, I am not sure she can protect them, even with a restraining order, as Jerry has already violated it without being arrested.

Our committee felt it imperative that I carefully document all meetings and interviews with the four family members and that you read my full report in order to get the complete benefit of everything I have learned in the course of my investigation. Will you let me know if you want to do that prior to the next court hearing? My report contains many more details of which you probably need to be aware.

I know this is a difficult case, but I believe that I have documented what we have been told by all parties as well as I could. I do not contend that one side is to blame for everything and the other side faultless, but I do not see the damage being inflicted by the mother at this time. Please let me know if you can be of any further assistance.

Very truly yours,
XXXX
Protective Services Worker
Child Protective Services

STANDING ON FAITH

With this report, finally things were beginning to turn in my favor, I thought. Even though I had evidence in my favor, I was always unsuccessful in winning any kind of victory in court against Jerry's powerful legal team, but his latest attack was the final blow. Jerry's legal defense successfully had the complete CPS findings and report sealed before it could be read in court. The CPS agent later told me that in 15 years of employment for CPS she had never, in the history of her career, been asked to do an investigation with a full report only to have her findings court-sealed and unread, with the judge apparently having never read her report. Jerry's allegations of child abuse against me looked more credible with each court hearing.

Just before my girls were taken from me, I trusted that God would intervene and deliver me from my impossible situation. I had chosen to stay in this abusive marriage standing on biblical promises that God would heal my 16-year marriage and that God would soften Jerry's abusive heart. I felt that I had done everything in my power to be in a position for God to deliver and bless me. Surely God would honor me for that, I felt.

None of this was what I envisioned for my destiny. My attitude had always been, "if I just loved my husband enough... if I were just good enough...if I just cleaned house enough... if I just tried to make myself pretty enough, he could find room in his heart to love me." Every attempt to try to hold my marriage together failed and eventually was nothing more than water running through my fingers. *Why then was it so hard for Jerry to simply love me?* I questioned myself.

In the years prior I was a home-school mother, Sunday school teacher, and a member on the small worship team at our church. If there was a way to be involved in the lives of my children, I did it and felt fulfilled in doing so. Once the girls went back to school, I volunteered my time by helping out on craft days or as a school lunch monitor. Seeing my involvement as an investment in my children's lives, I seldom turned down requests for help at the school or in the things that they were involved with and took on as many of their projects as I could. I devoted my days to being the best mother I could be.

FAMILY COURT SERVICES

One day in March of 1996, an announcement came over the loud speaker at my new job: "Ronda, please come to the front of the store." Two uniformed officers approached and informed me that both my daughters, then ages 8 and 12, had just been taken from me and placed in foster care because

I was being investigated. They told me that I was not in any way to look for the children and that the courts would be in contact with me shortly.

My world collapsed around me, and the walls spun around my head. *How could this be? I was the picture of a perfect mother—ask anyone,* I reasoned. My entire existence focused around my children's well-being.

"Pack small bags for both girls and drop them off with your attorney," they informed me.

My home was dark and abnormally still. The little cardboard fort that my girls were building lay abandoned just where they left it the night before. Their little nightgowns were piled on the edge of their beds where they had dressed for school. "Expect them to only be gone six weeks," the officers said, "while the investigation continues. Do not try to locate them!"

All visitations were to be court-supervised, and they allowed me only one precious hour each week jointly with the girls for which I had to pay $150 *per* visit. During our visits, I was forbidden to touch or hold the girls or be closer than the supervisor. She was court-ordered to transcribe each word I spoke for a detailed court report that followed my visit. During our visitation, my Lacie cried out for me to hold her, yet I could not, nor did they allow me to explain why they had to stay on the other side of the table from me. "All conversations were to be light and fluffy," I was warned. No explanations were given to my children; they were not informed why they were separated from me or why they could not touch me. My arms ached to console them as they cried and begged me to hold them.

While investigations of Jerry's latest allegations continued, his attorney demanded the appointment of an Amicus Attorney for both girls as well as independent psychologists for the girls and me, at my expense. What little I brought in from my minimum wage job went directly toward my rapidly increasing legal bills. Meanwhile money talked. With Jerry's vast financial resources, he hired one of the finest attorneys money could by, while I had to go with a "discount" lawyer.

The initial six-week abuse investigation quickly turned into months, and before long, I was in over my head in legal debt. While working a full-time job, I did not have the time or resources to respond to Jerry's lengthy bi-weekly legal accusations. Thus, his accusations went on the record as undisputed truth against me. My "not so discount" attorney was barraged with a legal battle he was unequipped to handle. When my divorce did later finalize, my case file was the largest divorce file in the history of that courthouse, extending over two volumes each several inches thick and it cost me well over $40,000, which I didn't have. Following our divorce, Jerry, who got the house, bragged to friends that his divorce cost him close to $250,000 in bribes and legal fees, when he had the house refinanced. I never knew if this was true or not.

ENDNOTE

1. The names of the girls have been changed to protect their privacy.

CHAPTER 4

AN UNHOLY ALLIANCE

During the last eight years of our marriage, Jerry and I changed churches to a smaller hometown non-denominational church. He was on the board, and I taught Sunday school and was on the worship team. Church staff embraced my outgoing and eager-to-assist personality and welcomed my involvement.

However, I was not aware of my husband's frequent meetings with the pastor just prior to our divorce in which Jerry convinced him of my supposed involvement in numerous adulterous affairs. Without my knowledge, he had taken the pastor on civilian "ride-alongs" while on patrol and told the pastor that I had contracted sexually transmitted diseases and was abusing our children. These were horrible untruths. The pastor or his staff never contacted me about these allegations, nor did they report me to the authorities as most people in such positions would and were required to do. Yet the pastor and his wife willingly agreed to testify against me in court. In exchange for their testimony, Jerry bestowed large personal offerings upon the church and even flew the family to Tennessee to purchase their middle child a horse to the tune of $1,500 plus the cost of transportation.

Jerry's plan to destroy me and to take away the children was completely premeditated. He knew exactly how to deceive the pastor and his wife and arranged every detail. In short, he traded my life and the lives of our children for the price of a horse.

A HORSE IN EXCHANGE FOR TESTIMONY

The pastor's middle daughter was my daughter Lillian's best friend. "Suzie"[1] spent much time at our house, even sometimes jokingly calling me "Mommy." When her mother found out about her nickname for me, she misunderstood, and Suzie's visits became much less frequent. Jerry felt he could rope the pastor's wife in because it appeared she already harbored feelings of bitterness in her heart. Because Suzie had spent so much time at our house, Jerry planned to get her to testify against me, to tell the courts that she had witnessed the alleged abuse. Her mother (the pastor's wife) was very willing to type up dozens of pages of affidavits and reports of abuse on behalf of her daughter, and she signed her daughter's name to them.

Both my daughters and Suzie shared a love of horses, and often I would take them out to go riding together. Lacie in particular loved horses and constantly toted around "Hershey," a brown plastic horse, her prized possession (the sole item she kept from her childhood), that to this day quietly rests tucked away in her closet. Our girls constantly begged us for horses of their own—and Jerry promised them that one day that would happen. He knew, of course, that Suzie also loved horses, and this would figure well into his scheme.

Jerry offered the pastor's family a horse for Suzie and paid to have the horse shipped to their home. He also gave the church huge offerings and paid for vacations for the pastor and his wife and several staff members.

The information regarding purchase of the horse was provided to the court authorities; however, the court dismissed any inappropriate actions regarding the pastor and his wife. When I questioned the judge in court about refusing to consider evidence that the pastor and his family might be dishonest or compromised, the judge simply looked me square and asked me, *"Why would a pastor lie?"*

The pastor and his family's testimony, therefore, stood against me as truth. There were no formal child abuse charges against me. Investigations by the family court and CPS determined I never harmed my children, yet on the basis of the pastor and his wife's hearsay and Jerry's testimony, they took my children from me.

Frankly, Jerry's lies did not come as a shock to me. Truth was not a strength or a priority in his life. After all of those years of living with him, I knew well his vengeance and retaliation. What did shock me was the violation of my pastor—of that one person you perceive as without flaw, the person (like a father figure) in a position of holy reverence and great trust. His false testimony opened me up to a new realm of mistrust, a new wave of rejection, and a new layer of raw woundedness. The pastor's untruthful testimony cut through my flesh and slashed a level of my soul I never knew existed. Every false allegation and "supposed" situation of abuse that he and his wife made in court and on paper, violated me to the core of who I was.

THE PASTOR'S UNTRUTHFUL TESTIMONY CUT THROUGH MY FLESH AND SLASHED A LEVEL OF MY SOUL I NEVER KNEW EXISTED

SUPERNATURAL MANIPULATION

Jerry's story is one of cunning, skillful manipulation, and cooperation with demonic influences. He strategically used everyone he could to manipulate circumstances and reposition situations to accomplish his ultimate goals. He was a man of power and influence, a great salesperson, and skilled in convincing people to do what he wanted. In the small town where we lived, he had been a wealthy and successful insurance/investment broker for many years and the police department's only Reserve Lieutenant. Setting himself up in the community as a volunteer in law enforcement and as a church board member made him *appear* influential and above the law, so that he could never be challenged for anything he did. His connections with the police and judicial system for 13 years afforded him many favors. Knowing the judges and attorneys well allowed him to take advantage of that system as needed. Extensive bribes and law enforcement connections guaranteed his success for any court hearing. He had always operated under a strong controlling spirit throughout our marriage; once he yielded himself completely to that controlling spirit, it became who he was near the end of our marriage.

As the investigation continued, our children remained in foster care. Through his connections, Jerry discovered where the girls were staying. After six months he was able to walk directly up to the foster care home and remove one of our daughters without any legal repercussions at all. He lied to the foster mother, boasting of having received full immediate custody of Lacie, and demanded that her things be packed and that he was taking only her that hour. They never thought to call the courts or ask for documents to verify his claims—they just packed her up and handed her to him. Nothing further was mentioned at court, and he was not required to return her or provide me with contact information.

On two occasions after Jerry took Lacie, I saw her by accident. The last time was when I ran into them at a restaurant. Jerry immediately jumped up from the table and screamed obscenities, hurling horrible filthy names across the restaurant while grabbing her and ushering her to the back of the room as though I was forbidden to see or touch her. Then he came after me with a violent vengeance. I raced out of the restaurant in fear.

From that point on, I lost all contact with her. It would be five years before I would see her again. In an attempt to keep her hidden from me during that time, he repeatedly dropped her off at the homes of strangers—single men—outside the county for weeks on end. She was shuffled from home to home with no explanations except the constant negative brainwashing he provided about how horrible I was; for her protection, he said, she would never see me again. He made her promise that if she ever saw me she would run away. Later she reported to me that he always kept a briefcase with thousands in cash, a loaded gun, and their passports to use if he needed. He would regularly discuss plans with her to "sneak away and live outside the country" should it be necessary.

Jerry's attorney was so efficient that I did not get alimony or support. I had no money, no real friends, no hope, and no life. After my herbal business was destroyed and our divorce began, I worked in a grocery store as a food demonstrator. The only food I had eaten for ten months (as the child-abuse investigation was underway) was what I could find in the salvage bins at the back of the grocery store. I lived on damaged or spoiled food and anything left over from the food demo I did that day. Day to day I never knew what or if I would eat. Looking back on it now, even that job was God's total grace upon me as it alone kept me fed for almost a year.

Thirteen years have passed since that time, yet even now I remember the many days I went hungry. Often I cannot enter a grocery store without being thankful for all God has done to restore me. The fact that I can actually buy anything I want to eat now is a constant reminder of God's goodness.

 *"IF THIS WAS THE BEST WAY GOD PROTECTS HIS CHILDREN...I WANT NO PART OF GOD!"*

FINALLY BROKEN

Soon after my children were put into foster care, I turned against God and blamed Him for not protecting me from Jerry in the first place and for not having judged my pastor and his family for the lies they told against me. Bitter that his church grew while I was dying on every level, I learned not to trust any living soul; I figured that given the right conditions, anyone would say anything for money.

When my children were taken in 1996, I walked out of my house, leaving everything as it was: dishes in the sink, laundry in the machine, toys strewn around, and their newly constructed cardboard fort in the living room. My home had become a morgue to me, a place that no longer welcomed my presence. The reminders of my children ripped such deep, bloody gashes in my heart that I simply could no longer live there. And so I left with the clothes on my back and slept anywhere I could to avoid having to return.

"If this was the best way God protects His children," I thought, *"I want no part of God!"* Angry and hurt beyond words, I spiraled down into a dangerous path of sin and destruction as a woman with a vendetta against God and a self-agenda of personal destruction. Now that life was completely meaningless, what was there left to live for?

Seven months after Lacie was taken, the courts were telling me that it was not *when,* but *if* I would ever get my oldest child, Lillian, back. (Lacie was already with Jerry.) Abuse investigations turned into an 11-month nightmare. Though Child Protective Services (CPS) and Family Court

Services (FCS) found absolutely *no* validity to Jerry's allegations that I abused my children, Lillian remained in the system. When I asked why I had no parental rights with either of my children, they told me that Jerry's expert eyewitness (the pastor) testified that he had both seen and had firsthand knowledge of the abuse, which substantiated Jerry's allegations.

By the beginning of 1997, suicide fantasies danced daily before my eyes. Jerry had overlooked one loaded gun when he left, and I thought it was my ticket out. However at the time I lacked the courage to pull the trigger, so I changed my death wish to alcohol with hopes that I could drink my way into my own fatal car accident to end a long history of disappointments and regrets. Massive consumption of alcohol, however, only temporarily dulled my pain and failed to bring the results I desired. Sleep eluded me because it was during the midnight hours that my mind raced with the painful memories of a life no longer available to me. I partied hard every night and would work every day, trying to fill the void left by my missing children. During the time my children remained in foster care, I seldom ate because I really didn't have much food, and I lost 65 pounds, dropping from a dress size 12 to a size 1.

How had my life ended up in such a mess? Everything I touched seemed to self-destruct, and I was isolated and emotionally lost with death at the forefront of my daily longings. If only I had the courage to pull the trigger of the gun...how easy it would have been for me. Sitting in the emptiness of my mind, I remembered the things I held so dear and how violently they were taken from me—in the blink of an eye—my whole life and reason for living, now gone. Completely gone.

Could it get any worse? I couldn't imagine it but it did. Despite all investigations having cleared me from any wrongdoing, Lillian remained in foster care. Eleven months she'd been there—we'd been apart for so long. I had been absolved of all negative accusations, and she should have been in my arms at home, yet the courts contacted me to say that I was about to lose *all* parental rights. The foster family wanted to pursue legal adoption, and I was legally powerless to stop it.

I had no idea where Lacie was, and I was now in the process of losing all parental rights of Lillian as well. In an instant and without warning they were ripped from my arms. Their sudden abduction by the State felt exactly like a kidnapping to me. It had been five months since I had seen Lacie or had any knowledge of her health or welfare. Never did I have the chance to say good-bye to her or tell either child why things were happening or how they had happened. Life lost all meaning and purpose for me.

Rage and hatred seethed inside me like a wildfire or a terminal cancer. I despised men in general, and those especially in positions of power within corrupt systems: attorneys, law enforcement, the judicial system, religion.

SURRENDER

I was through with church, religion, leadership, family, and authority, for they had all failed and destroyed me—every shred of trust and hope in the church and in the justice system shriveled. Burned up and burned out, I'd had enough. If sin was pleasant for a season, even that season lost all luster. My party friends didn't even want to hang out with me because I was "too sad" for them; I "hampered" their party with my constant dismal countenance which alcohol couldn't even lift. Shunned on every level and at my own personal ground zero, I was determined that it was to be my last day of work—the last day of my life.

It was lunchtime, and I couldn't wait to walk the beach one last time before I ended everything. Finally I mustered the courage to die. Life was over.

ENDNOTE

1. Name changed to protect her.

PART II

THE

BEGINNING

CHAPTER 5

AND THERE WAS WAR
IN HEAVEN

I just wanted death, and desired it quickly—never mind the details. Was there really anything beyond death? Hell was my life, and whatever was beyond as an alternative was better. I wanted nothing more to do with God or the church. Both had let me down. My heart felt as cold as the steel gun resting in my hand. Hatred filled and permeated every fiber of my being. Nobody cared—even God. All was for naught. Freedom was just a trigger pull away.

The waves lapped gently upon the deserted shore as though inviting me to the water's edge. My season of desolation was over. My life a shambles—death would bring me instant peace. Change was on its way—but not the way I had planned it.

"Ronda..." someone called in a voice loud enough to shake the heavens. It startled me—there was no one on the

beach and there was no way someone's voice could travel so clearly over the sound of the wind and ocean.

"Ronda..." the audible, powerful voice said again. Strangely enough, it felt like a fresh wind of hope against my face. *"If you will trust Me, I will put the pieces of your broken life back together again."*

"IF YOU WILL TRUST ME, I WILL PUT THE PIECES OF YOUR BROKEN LIFE BACK TOGETHER AGAIN."

It had to be God—it could be no other. For I don't know how long, God spoke to my heart and revealed things only He could know. He told me that He knew of my anger toward Him for permitting things to happen in my life, for what I perceived as His lack of protection and justice on my behalf. Almost instantly He revealed to my heart the hurts of many years when I trusted Him to protect me, yet felt He had singled me out to suffer and had rejected me as well.

"Yes, I hate You—I hate You with all that is within me!" I screamed into the heavens, my hatred surfacing and flashing like lightning through every part of me, and from the very depths of my heart. Deeply ingrained hatred and mistrust boiled through my bones and coursed through my lips at the speed of light, exposing deep-seated feelings of betrayal and rejection toward God and society. Realizing this shocked and surprised even me.

How could this be? I wondered. I had loved the Lord all of my life—I raised my children to love Him, to know and trust Him. How could I come to hate the God whom I'd worshiped since childhood? But I knew He was right. I did not trust Him because I felt He'd always let me down. It would have been easy for Him to step in and rescue me in a heartbeat, to bring my father back to me, or to stop the abuse, or to give me back my girls. If He really cared, why didn't He show it then—why now when I was in the final moment of life?

Audibly again, He restated, *"Ronda. I will put the pieces of your broken life together if you will trust Me."* But how could He after all of *my* recent poor choices—my life was a disaster. Without my children—life wasn't worth picking up and repairing.

Somehow He ignited new hope in my heart. Crying, I fell on my knees in the sand and begged God's forgiveness.

"Forgive me, Father, for hating You. I don't hate You. Forgive me for my poor choices of this past year. Please put my life back together. I don't think You can, but if You will, I'll serve You all the days of my life."

As desperately as I had wanted to die, I suddenly wanted to live with Him if He was in the picture. Suddenly hope rose in me like a tide. Heaven breathed the holy breath of God's DNA into my brokenness, and life swirled around and within me making me feel lighter, rejuvenated by His love. For the first time in my life, I sincerely felt that I would live to declare the glory of the Lord. I would not die, and my children and I would be OK; everything would work out for good for our lives. It was the most empowering moment of my existence. I don't think I'd ever really made salvation mine until that moment. For me to walk in victory, this renewed decision to glorify God with my life required serious life changes.

There on the seashore, the Holy Spirit immediately illuminated Scripture from Second Chronicles 7:14:

If My people who are called by My name will humble themselves, and pray and seek My face, and turn from their wicked ways, then I will hear from heaven, and will forgive their sin and **heal their land** (NKJV).

My devastation and losses, my lack of will to live, hurled me into a life of sin that last year. He showed me that for Him to rebuild my life, I'd have to turn and walk away from the sinful acts. For sure I wanted to give the Lord every opportunity to rebuild and restore! I made an immediate heart decision, repented, and promised to turn away from the old life and go forward into the new. Never would I turn or even look back again.

Death had no foothold. Life was the victor. I left the sandy battleground triumphant and in new relationship with the Lord. Every weight lifted, the burdens seemed light, and I felt cleansed and restored.

Desiring now a truly godly life, I knew I could not risk the lure of compromise. So upon returning to work, I went straight to the office and gave my resignation notice, as my party friends were also my co-workers. God also instantly delivered me from my recently acquired desire for alcohol, and I forged ahead into my new life. Every decision I made to cut the ties that bound me brought new levels of freedom and unspeakable joy. To know just how much God loved me— that He would give me such a tangible and real encounter with Him—well, it was joy unspeakable and glorious.

Instant transformation is possible with God! He can change us in an instant! He stepped into my misery and injected me with hope. Here I was, angry, resentful, bitter, filthy, broken, dirty, and void of emotion, and He did not punish me. How merciful He was to create a new life within me! He reached out of Heaven and sent rivers of healing love that still reverberate in the depths of my heart. I was a true prodigal—saved by His grace and compassion.

COURAGE

God gave me the courage to return to my house which I'd vacated because I couldn't face the painful memories. When the girls were taken away, I closed everything up—leaving everything as it was. It had been months since I'd been in their bedroom, and I had to literally walk through cobwebs to enter, which intensified the pain of my loss. Their clothes and nightgowns still lay piled on the bed where they left them, as though time had stood still. Sitting on their bed in an awkward quiet moment, my heart grieved and pined for their return. Yet I didn't feel as hopeless now—new faith kindled in my heart. Seeing their belongings brought back the reality of the pain I had tried to escape with alcohol, but now I was sober and trusting God for restoration, the fulfillment of His promise to me.

Nevertheless, I still felt the intense pain of missing them, and pulling a wool blanket over my head, I lay down on the sofa and cried myself to sleep. In my sleep the Lord gave me a dream. I saw an octagon-shaped, spinning display case suspended from the ceiling with separations. Each separation was filled with beautiful things. One separation had a home, one had a car, one had a business, and the last had children. A note rested on the bottom of the case that read, "Everything in here I will give to you if you trust in Me." Then I heard the Lord speak to my heart this verse:

> *Delight yourself also in the Lord, and He shall give you the desires of your heart* (Psalm 37:4 NKJV).

God's restoration began immediately and has faithfully continued to this day. Where once I thought that He was against me—now I know He was always lovingly for me. I had every confidence that He would turn everything around.

CHAPTER 6

TESTING

Two difficult weeks passed, yet I was just as determined to walk out my decisions as I had been the first day. Though nothing much changed in my situation, I believe that during those two *long* and painful, sober weeks God was testing my heart to determine if I would remain committed to my repentance. On the upside, my mother and I enjoyed a sweet time of healing as God restored our relationship.

On the downside, Jerry, consumed with hatred, was still stalking me and had just that week tried again to intimidate me by closely driving wildly behind me in an effort to cause me to get in an auto accident or run my car off the road. Several friends of his had called again with intimidating messages. My job was ending, and I had no idea where I would go to work or what I would do for money. Legal bills were mounting. I went back to the same place the Lord had met me two weeks prior and cried aloud, *"Lord, You and I both know that Jerry is going to kill me. I am so afraid. Can You please help me?"* No audible voice this time—no tangible presence—but I left the beach hopeful. Within a few weeks after that prayer, the Lord did send me a special someone whom He used greatly to begin to heal the broken fragments of my heart.

NEW JOB OPPORTUNITIES

Before long, restoration was becoming visible in most areas of my life. Within days of my old job ending, an old friend who had tried for weeks to contact me finally did—with a wonderful job opportunity. A new company was looking for a spokesperson to travel, all expenses paid, all over the United States to promote a new, alternative health product. The job paid $500 per weekend—for one lecture. Of course I took the job.

ONE CHILD RESTORED

Only six weeks after my God encounter, the courts contacted me and informed me that the foster care parents who had Lillian had suddenly changed their minds about the adoption and the courts were returning her to my *full* custody. I could hardly believe it. I could just go to the court and pick her up. Understand, it was hard to believe that it could be as easy as that, especially after all I'd been through to even visit her much less regain custody rights. I'd spent tens of thousands of dollars in court and for visitation rights. I'd been through hell and back, and now without even a flutter of an eyelash, I could just go and pick her up without a court hearing, an explanation, or an apology—just a "have-a-nice-life" attitude. It was all so confusing, but I wasn't about to stop and question things.

I sped to get her and brought her home for a joyful reunion! Later I learned that the foster care parents stopped the adoption proceedings because my daughter had developed a crush on their pre-teen hormonal son, and it was not what they had bargained for. God works His ways so splendidly. This was a supernatural miracle.

FINANCIAL RESTORATION

Financial restoration came by way of God through a unique source as well when someone handed me a check and said, "Here, re-open your herbal business!" As grateful as I was, I was unsure if it was even possible because when Jerry destroyed everything, I lost the formulas. However, the Lord directed me to call the manufacturer who had bottled my formulas, and it turned out that they'd saved all of the data. I promptly quit my traveling job and began production of the four herbal formulations previously supernaturally given to me, and I successfully launched www.Re-Nue.com, an Internet business. Things were slow the first few years as I started from scratch again, but the Lord eventually turned things around, providing for me through this renewed business beyond my expectations.

Just as God promises in His Word to restore sevenfold, so He did in our lives. Everything I ever dreamed of, He granted and delighted in giving me in abundance. He restored what the locust destroyed. I want to encourage you. God really does love to give His children the desires of their hearts. He actually looks for ways to bless us when we walk in obedience to His Word.

CHAPTER 7

GIVING ACCOUNT

Lillian had only been home for six weeks, and it was our first Christmas together since the custody nightmare began. A knock on the door Christmas Eve 1997 yielded a subpoena to appear in court. Jerry had filed a "defamation of character" lawsuit against me for $2 million—and I have no doubt that he planned the notice delivery on Christmas Eve on purpose.

His lawsuit claimed that this defamation, which was really just me sharing with two friends things that had happened, caused his deteriorating health condition as a result of his long, ongoing battle with hepatitis C. Interestingly, he also filed an identical lawsuit against Child Protective Services for their investigations against him, which he alleged also contributed to his decline. He was going against the entire system in an all-out attempt to cover up, in my opinion, his own evil misdoings. This was a standard proactive aggression and combative assault pattern of his—coming after people who opposed him aggressively before they had a chance to come after him for his misconduct.

As ridiculous as his claims were, I still had to fight them, but I could not afford any more legal fees. I contacted a number of lawyers, but no one wanted to represent me because I had no money.

"What would happen if I didn't fight this?" I asked one lawyer.

"You'll lose by default, he'll be awarded the judgment, and you'll be paying him the rest of your life." They said that anyone can file a lawsuit against another person, at will, for any reason.

I could not afford an attorney, but I also could not afford to lose, so I laid it all in the hands of the Lord and His intervention. I prayed, "Lord, this miracle, please open a door..." and I believed, because since the rededication of my heart on the beach, my new life had become a miracle. Well, God seemed to rise up and say, "Enough is enough!" Although the enemy had reared in an all-out attempt to steal again, the Spirit of the Lord was about to raise a standard against him to halt every method of attack.

I contacted one more attorney who gave me hope. Here was a different report. "Did the spousal abuse happen in your home?" he asked.

"Why, yes...yes, it did."

"Your homeowner's insurance will cover your legal defense expenses then," he said, "as long as you have a police report and restraining order against your ex-husband."

It was unheard of—something I never would have thought possible. Imagine a homeowner's insurance company paying for legal defense. They agreed and assigned a legal team as we began another long task of courtroom battle. Jerry had money, lots of it. Money buys power. Power buys people. Jerry assimilated a team of loyal buddies including police officers who were ready to testify against me. This unnerved my attorneys; they did not want to face his crew. I demanded a trial by jury, as clearly this entire trial was a mockery and travesty of justice, but my insurance company-appointed attorneys denied my request in favor of looking out for their own best interests: understandable, but hard to take. Just before we were to go to final hearing, and against my pleading not to settle, they settled out of court for $30,000. Though I was not involved in the CPS lawsuit, I believe they also settled out of court. Jerry promptly took the $30,000 and purchased himself a snappy, red Nissan 300ZX.

TIME FOR A CHANGE

He continued stalking me and threatening me with bodily harm. He just wouldn't quit in his relentless pursuit. Finally a door opened for us to move to Houston, Texas. After the move, we did not hear again from Jerry. It had been a difficult year, as I struggled financially. I found myself emotionally devastated with little to offer and owing everyone. Even though God was, thankfully, blessing us all of the time, I'd brought into my new life much yet-to-be-healed woundedness and debt.

My mother's illness was worsening by ovarian cancer. She was so close to death that hospice warned us that it could be any day for her. It was a hard road—for her and for all of us, mentally and physically. Months of watching her body waste away while walking with her through excruciating pain left me drained and weary. Though I was thankful that Lillian could spend time bonding with Grandma, my heart deeply grieved that Lacie would never know her grandmother who dearly loved her.

 *"...RIGHT NOW YOUR MOTHER IS STANDING BEFORE ME GIVING ACCOUNT. WHAT HAVE YOU EVER DONE FOR ME?"*

It was very late as I nodded off on the makeshift pallet I had at the foot of her bed. Her cats were unusually active and noisy this night—obviously agitated. Glancing at my mother, it was obvious that we were losing her—that she was in the last moments of her life. Leaping to her side, I grabbed her lifeless body to hold her as she released her last and final breath. I recall thinking that it was such a long, endless breath—it went on and on and on.

Time stood still for what seemed an eternity, and the Lord spoke audibly to me, for the second time in my life.

"Ronda, right now your mother is standing before Me giving account. What have you ever done for Me?" It was a moment instantly defined with the complete knowledge of the full

intention of His question. Indeed, what had I done? Almost my entire lifetime I had attended church, yet I had lacked any depth of spiritual intimacy, growth, or power. The volume and magnitude of His question released wave after wave of disappointments that reached to the heart of my inner soul. *"Nothing..."* I pondered, *"nothing..."* How could 37 years have been so wasted on meaningless, trivial pursuits? Yes, I had a salvation experience with Jesus. Yes, I attended church regularly. Yes, I tried to the best of my ability to live a godly life. But I instantly realized I had nothing substantially attributed to my account in Heaven. Not one salvation.

Begging God's forgiveness, I vowed to Him that following the funeral, I would pursue His will for my life. I was not sure where to begin or what it would look like, but I knew that the rest of my life had to be devoted to doing His will, whatever that was.

I would soon find out.

Mom's dear friend Patricia and her husband Argis were involved in a prison chaplain program. During her visits to mom, she shared how personally satisfying it was to minister to inmates. The job required no special skills or training, just a love of the Lord and a desire to share His love with others.

I can do that! My heart leapt as a gazelle—and her suggestion instantly felt true in my heart, as if it had always been my calling. The following month I began my training to become a prison chaplain's assistant, and then completed a chaplain's certification within the prison system itself.

Still, I didn't feel adequate or qualified enough to minister to others. Nevertheless, the first two years of my prison ministry I spent twice weekly in the chaplain's office as a volunteer counselor to the female inmates. My job was to deliver the news when a loved one died, and although it was a difficult duty, it always amazed me how the sweet presence of the Lord would come in and minister to each hurting woman's heart. In almost every case, our grief counseling session turned into an opportunity for salvation and baptism of the Holy Spirit. I saw hundreds of women saved and baptized in the Holy Spirit during those two years.

Later I transferred to another prison unit; and instead of counseling, the Lord had me preaching weekly, with signs, wonders, and miracles following! It was truly a supernatural time with many salvations. The sweet presence of the Lord wooed me into a deeper relationship with Him. Even though I had no grid for understanding what I was experiencing in Him, I did understand just how hungry I was for His presence—and I never had enough of Him. My appetite for His presence and for relationship grew and grew and grew.

CHAPTER 8

DON'T CRY

During this wonderful season of restoration, I enjoyed waves of God's glory and His manifested presence through tremendous times of intimacy with much healing and deliverance. It was at this time that the Lord gave me a personal promise to return my youngest daughter Lacie to me, and it came by way of the Book of Jeremiah.

> *The Lord spoke to me again, saying: In Ramah there is bitter weeping, Rachel* [I changed it to Ronda in my Bible] *is weeping for her children* [Lacie] *and she cannot be comforted, for they are gone. But the Lord says: Don't cry any longer, for I have heard your prayers and you will see them again; they will come back to you from the distant land of the enemy. There is hope for your future, says the Lord, and your children will come again to their own land* (Jeremiah 31:15-17 TLB).

Five years had passed since I had seen her last, yet my heart still pined to have Lacie back in my life. I had no contact with her and no idea where she was. For several years the Lord had been dealing with me about beginning to write this very book.

"But I can't, Lord," I argued, "the last chapter hasn't happened yet…she's still not home."

He answered me by way of a prophetic word one Sunday during the worship service at church. *"My time of waiting was over,"* the prophet told me. I knew the Lord referred to my daughter! I could hardly wait, and when I got home, I half expected a message already waiting from Jerry whom I heard had since remarried. But days turned into weeks, turned into months. I took that prophetic word of the Lord and engaged in warfare, determined to get my promise. The spirit of intercession roared inside of me, and then the Lord supernaturally showed me, word for word, how to pray. He gave me the exact words to pray! "Pray only those words," He commanded.

Jerry's health began to significantly decline following our divorce. His new wife felt very threatened by Lacie's presence and any claim she may have to Jerry's vast financial empire. Therefore Jerry's new wife only wanted Lacie gone.

I prayed the specific prayer the Lord had instructed me to for a few more weeks—until I got *the* call.

A voice on the other end said: "Jerry has pulled a gun on his new wife, threatening to kill both her *and* you. She walked out on him and asked me to call you. Here's your daughter's address…"

After restarting my herbal business, God had breathed on it for a second time, and by this point it was again extremely successful. With Lacie's new contact information, I was on the next plane, cash in hand for the new attorney. Things were going to be different now. I would be successful. Laying all of the money on a high-priced, fancy attorney's desk once I arrived, I commanded, "Go and get my daughter!" She filed immediate motions, and I was awarded unsupervised visitation three days out of the week during a time of *reunification* (the court called it) of two weeks. Upon completion if all went well, I would get full custody. Initially, Lacie, who was now 12 years of age, was terrified to see me, having been brainwashed by those she trusted as her caregivers. She screamed and cried in fear and terror when I showed up with the legal documents in my favor. Instinctively I came prepared for a battle and requested an escort by three patrol cars upon my first visitation. I would not be denied again! This was *my* season, and I would not leave without my Lacie, and no devil in hell would stop me this time.

Jerry was now gravely sick with complications extending from his liver transplant. Lacie had been taken to a friend of Jerry's. I was instructed to wait by my rental car as the first two patrol units delivered my court order for visitation to Lacie's unwilling host. The scene turned frightening as he began to scream at me that I was not going to get her. Lacie, by now terrified, screamed, "You can't make me go!" The first two patrol officers returned to me and said that they were unwilling to physically pull her out of the house. I began to pray beside my car and asked God for yet another miracle. When I saw the third patrol unit, I approached him and told him my story, explaining the facts and details surrounding my daughter's abduction, and I could see compassion in his eyes as he listened intently to my story. The officer, in fact, resolved that I would not leave that day without seeing my daughter.

"You leave this to me, and don't worry," he whispered, looking at me directly. He told me to stay at the car no matter what, "I will get your girl!" he reassured. My heart raced with excitement. I was as determined as a mother lion going in for the final kill to protect her cub.

Against the wishes of the first two patrol units, this compassionate officer took my court order and headed for the door determined to succeed no matter the cost. He told me later what happened next. When he entered the chaotic house, he confronted the man. He told him that I was the mother and that legally he was powerless to stop me from getting my child because I held all legal rights and was in a financial position to powerfully execute a barrage of legal attacks upon him if he opposed me further. The officer informed him also that he would be taking Lacie with or without his consent as per the order of the court, and to prepare her things for the visitation. Lacie screamed her objection and fear as the officer reached for her hand. He led her outside and to me and she reluctantly got in the car and off we went. She was scared and frightened and stared out the window as I attempted to explain what happened, that I had been searching for her and fighting a legal battle to see her since she was taken from us, and how I never stopped loving her. She was shocked to learn this as she had been told daily that I hated her and had her sent away, and that her present living conditions were again my fault.

Five years of the daily brainwashing into believing how horrible and dangerous I was...Yet it only took about one hour for me to get the breakthrough we needed to begin rebuilding our relationship. We spent the next few hours tearfully holding each other, hugging, and talking like mother and child as God's miracle-working power began powerfully restoring everything the enemy stole from me. By the end of the two weeks, we were beginning to enjoy a mother-daughter relationship. She was writing homemade cards and letters to me, which I submitted to the court as evidence to substantiate the fact that reunification was successful. They awarded me *full* custody! I picked up her things in my rental car, and we drove straight back to Texas to be with Lillian!

Although no one informed me until almost a month after the fact, several weeks after I received full custody, neighbors found Jerry, who had just returned home from the hospital, alone and unconscious on his floor. He was hospitalized again from complications of hepatitis C and liver-related problems and died shortly afterward. Sadly, his friends reported to me that in the end, Jerry was still angrily cursing God and refused any ministry toward repentance when he died. As per his will, Jerry's new wife became the sole inheritor to his vast estate. He did not remember Lillian or Lacie in his will, nor were they informed of his death or invited to his funeral. His wife wanted nothing to do with his girls and went so far as to refuse Lacie even a photograph of her father to remember him by. History again repeated itself; as it was for me with my father, they also had no real closure regarding his death.

Both girls were deeply hurt and emotionally damaged because of the divorce, their separation, and the confirmed traumatic incidents of his abuse and others that followed. Likewise, both girls have a dynamic testimony of their own. The Lord has spoken to both of them about writing their stories one day. I have purposely left out the details of the girls' experiences as I feel that their stories are theirs alone to tell. God continues to move, bringing healing to both their hearts and restoring the years they lost. Their separation and trauma caused damage beyond calculation, but God remains faithful. I stand on His promise that because He started a good work in our lives, He will be faithful to complete it and that in the end all things do work together for our good.

CHAPTER 9

CALLED TO MINISTRY

I had little understanding of the prophetic, having only seen it in very limited examples a few times in my life. But my life forever changed when a minister friend looked at me one day and said, "Ronda, girl, you have *no* idea the call of God on your life."

I sat there shocked and stunned! *Did I hear him correctly? Me? Why in all of heaven would God use me? What in the world did I have that was so unique or valuable to God?* I wondered. I argued in my heart that I knew dozens of persons more qualified for ministry than myself. I had been weekly with the prison system for two years now but never really considered that a *ministry*. Sharing about the love of Jesus and the goodness of God became something I loved to do.

"RONDA, GIRL, YOU HAVE NO IDEA THE CALL OF GOD ON YOUR LIFE."

I asked him to repeat himself as if I had not heard him the first time. He just looked at me and smiled. Never before had the concept ever occurred to me that the Lord could use me for anything substantial for the Kingdom. I begged my friend to tell me what he knew; what had he heard the Lord say? His quiet smile only frustrated me further. He knew something. I was sure of it. Why would he not tell me?

I determined that coming weekend to start my very first fast. I wanted to see what he saw, know what he knew. I figured an aggressive three-day fast would provide an answer. Purposely locking myself in my bedroom, I recall my frustration as I prayed for hours, begging God to reveal to me *"if"* I had a call upon my life. No one coached or mentored me in fasting or in calling on God for specifics—I didn't know what to expect, nor did I have any understanding for what I was about to see or experience.

Day one—nothing. Day two—nothing. As day three rolled around, I grew more frustrated, unsure that I was even hearing God's voice much less doing anything else correctly. Old feelings of rejection by God began to surface within my heart. The sun was setting on the last day of my fast, just as I laid my Bible on the floor and stretched myself out atop of it, crying out to God like never before. While in a dream-like state, I began to see something. What was happening? Had I perhaps fallen asleep?

I saw myself standing on a large platform, with a large audience crammed in the meeting area. The front rows were full of invalids and people in wheelchairs. As I preached, a light beamed from my mouth, eyes, ears, and hands. When I finished preaching, I walked off the platform, grabbed a man in a wheelchair, and pulled him up out of the chair.

MEETING MAMIE

Without understanding I rose from the floor and sat there pondering what I had seen. As I was wondering if I had made it up, the phone rang. It was the very same minister friend who had spoken into my life three days earlier. I told him what I thought I had seen and if he could explain what was going on in me. He recommended that I contact a dear woman who had mentored him in his ministry, and he gave me her phone number.

I called her right away and explained what I thought I had seen and asked her to consider mentoring me. She explained that her life was currently very full with no extra time for much else; however, she told me she would pray about it and get back to me. The next day Mamie did call back and told me that during prayer the Lord began to show her things similar to what I had seen. Then the Lord told her that she was to mentor me, and that there was purpose in it.

Within a week Mamie started to meet with me, lovingly teaching and instructing me in the deeper things of the Spirit. While studying the Bible together, she taught me things like how to pray effectively, how to intercede, how to war, and how to press into a deeper level of worship. Our prayer times took us many places in the Spirit. After several weeks Mamie began introducing me to very prophetic ministers who would pray and prophesy direction over my life. With each prophecy having similar characteristics of a healing ministry and a strong teaching anointing, it was not long before I had a clearer understanding of what the Lord desired to do in and through my life. Then I started dreaming of a healing anointing.

I began to understand that there was a call of God upon my life. This concept greatly baffled my mind. *Why would God want to use me?* I pondered again and again. A million other more qualified people could do a much better job. Yes, I could provide God with their references. I just didn't feel qualified.

I spent many hours arguing with the Lord and trying to talk Him out of using me, until one pivotal day when He spoke very sternly and sharply to my heart this warning, *"Ronda, I tell you the truth, you will cry bitter tears when you stand before My throne if you do not fulfill all I have destined for you to do. You need to embrace the anointing and mantles I have put on your life and fulfill the call that is before you."* Therefore, from that day forward, I decided in my heart to complete my God-ordained, predestined assignment, to stop running from His will, and to allow His Spirit to take me wherever He needed to in order to submit to His plans and purposes. Once this word was spoken over my life, I desired its fullness in greater depth.

But there was much more healing and deliverance needed before I could be that holy vessel that He could pour His Spirit upon, and I determined to cooperate with the Holy Spirit, setting my face like flint to begin the process of healing and recovery. I desperately wanted to be used.

I explored and studied the teachings of an evangelist who was experiencing creative miracles. Deciding I needed to see for myself, I drove 12 hours to sit in on one of his meetings. I was one of the first to be called up and given a direct word confirming my past, present, and future events. He began to speak of the struggles and intense warfare that had made up portions of who I was—the hurts and pains that gave me both a dramatic personal testimony and memories I had spent a lifetime trying to forget.

THE EVANGELIST'S PROPHETIC WORD

Come, Holy Spirit. I want this lady in the blue jacket to stand up. Now what is your name again? [Ronda.] Ronda, right, is that what it is? OK, just lift your hands up.

Holy Spirit, come right now in the name of Jesus. Father, release Your power. Father, release Your presence in the name of Jesus.

Now there's a warfare that's been against you. The church, religion, and leadership, the things that have taken place. You've been through a season of testing and trials. But you said, "God, this isn't just of Your hand," and you said the devil has to be in this thing because of how long you have wandered in this dry and thirsty land, where there is no water, and you're hungry for the fresh touch, the release of the gift that you know God has put into your life.

There is a release of ministry that God has for you, and I believe that He is saying, "There is an end of one season. The winter is passed…it is spring." I see the turning of a new page. I see the opening of a new chapter for you. And God is going to begin to take you out of that place that you are in now and set you on your high hills.

There is a real sovereign place of the coming of the Lord. Like an eagle, He is going to begin to carry you upon the wings of an eagle, and you are just beginning to soar. And you are going to find the Lord placed you in the place He has called you.

And the Lord has given you permission. It is like the Lord is saying, "I have put something in your hands—do it!" And there is permission for you to begin to move forward.

And though there is apprehension and though there is fear, the Lord is going to begin to remove the oppositions that are against you and cause there to be a highway.

There is a preparing. There is a prepared way for you in the spirit, and I believe there is a permission, and there is a grace, and there is a favor.

And I believe there is a release over you from some former things. A release over you from some things that have kept you tethered down and have kept you in a state of confusion. There is a cloud of confusion over your mind, and the wind of God's Spirit is going to release you right now.

And there is clarity of vision coming because you are a discerner. You are one that sees. You are one that knows. But there has been a cloudiness. There's been a lack of hearing and your understanding has been dull. And you haven't been able to get the breakthrough. But God's going to restore the vision and God's going to bring you out—*tried, tested, true,* and *faithful!*

And there's going to be reward. God is a rewarder of those who diligently seek Him. And there's reward for you right now. There's blessing for you right now.

The devil wants to come kill, steal, and destroy, and it is the warfare you have walked through. But I want to declare the victory of the Lord of Hosts over you and your life, right now in the name of Jesus. We release victory for her. We say victory is mine. That is what the Lord is releasing to you right now is the victory.

You are going to walk through some things, beginning to take place now. Even in your circumstances, and in your situation, in the midst of the impossibility. The storms around you are huge. That which is piled up against you, the opposition, the circumstances, the mountains of impossibility, the hindrance, and opposition to what God said.

But it is, *Who are you, oh mountain; you shall become a plain.* And so I see the coming of the Lord making things a plain for you. Lifting you up...the rough places, and making them smooth for you, bringing the mountains low, lifting the valleys high.

You are coming up out of the valley with a new anointing. Because when Jesus came up out of the wilderness, He came up out in the power of the Spirit, and so there's a new power of God's Spirit that is going to be on you for the things of ministry, 'cause there's a preaching mantle on you.

I see treasures in you. I see the treasure of the Kingdom, the treasure of wisdom, and the treasure of knowledge. And you're coming out with that treasure, that preaching and that teaching.

And there have been parts of your life that you have said, "God, I can't even do that because of where I am, and who I am. I don't even feel like I have anything to give." It is like you have said, "Oh my God, there's a little jar of oil and there's a little bit of flour." But God said, "I have put something in your hands, and I want you to use it. I have put something in you, and I want you to do it," and God's going to bring an understanding of that. Even in a greater way, in the name of Jesus.

God's blessings are on you. His favor is on you. There's a release on you. There's a grace on you, and the Lord of Hosts is coming against your battles. The Lord of Hosts is coming against the warfare, in the name of Jesus. So, Holy Spirit, let it come now. Thank You, Lord.

As he spoke about the woman with the measured amount of oil and flour, I stood there shocked; I had used that exact analogy with the Lord in times past. No one could have known that.

I felt empowered in the months following this powerful prophetic word. In so many areas of my life I felt as if I never really had understanding or closure. My life had consisted of what continually felt like the recurrent tearing of my heart. I felt no one really understood my secret pain and loss until this word. The Lord confirmed to me that He knew the pain. He saw the abuse. That everything I had suffered— the reproach and the betrayal—would not be meaningless, but would be used for His glory. Through this word, He confirmed to me that the enemy had greatly come against me in his attempt to destroy me. I felt the Lord reach out, like a loving compassionate Father might do, and hold me and tell me everything would be OK. Instead of always feeling isolated, I felt heard and understood for the first time in a long time.

LOVE THROUGH THE EYES OF THE LORD

For most of my life, I had entertained a very warped sense of love. I patterned love after those things I could touch or that I thought to be true. I understood love through the example shown to me by those closest to me, who claimed to love me. However, in most cases, I came to understand that sadly, earthly love is not a true pattern or example of the degree of love God has for us.

My parents, my ex-husband, and at times my own children could only love me on an earthly level. And more often than not, that love proved to be extremely conditional, emotional, judgmental, punishing, and in some cases downright cruel. Sure, there were seasons or glimpses of kinder love, but nothing I had ever experienced could compare to the love God has for us.

At times it can be difficult, without a measure of faith and inner healing, to understand the realms of pure, unconditional, godly love when you have experienced years of rejection by those you trusted to love you. Rejection from a loved one seems to cut to the very core of a person and, in many cases, leaves scars so deep that the Lord alone is the only one who has the ability to heal them.

I've heard people talk on the subject of godly love, but I had a difficult time coming to understand why God would desire to love me personally. Rather, I had always thought that God was a God of judgment waiting for and anticipating any opportunity to bring punishment to me for my many sins. I had a lifetime of listening to the lies of the enemy that said that my sins were "too many for the love of the Lord to cover." I could see the love of the Lord for others but inwardly doubted the sincerity of that love as available for myself. I clearly saw God's physical healing for others yet doubted its availability for me personally.

Throughout my life I often asked, *"Lord, if You really loved me, how could You have allowed this person to hurt me and abuse me the way he did?"* I balanced God's protection and God's love on the same scale and concluded that God's apparent lack of protection for me had to mean that He was also limited in His ability to love me for whatever reason.

...EACH MAN WILL INDIVIDUALLY ANSWER TO HIM FOR THE WAY HE LOVES, PROTECTS, OR MISHANDLES HIS GOD-GIVEN AUTHORITY...

For years I judged God's love based upon my own opinions, hurts, and abandonment and rejected any ability to receive His love, based solely upon my own ungodly belief system.

Through His love for me, He began to reveal the mysteries of how and why unmerited, undeserved abuse at the hands of others is allowed to happen. He showed me that He honors authority in the family, that He has given man authority over his own family, and each man will individually answer to Him for the way he loves, protects, or *mishandles* his God-given authority through abuse against his family members, loved ones, and those whom he has been given authority over.

I began asking Him to show me how and why He loves me. He showed me that nothing could separate me from His holy love. He consistently reaffirmed His love to me. The examples He used amazed me. A prophetic friend handed me an extremely delicious-smelling candle one day. When I enquired why, she said the Lord told her to give it and tell me this wonderful fragrance is how He sees me, that my praise was His wonderful fragrance.

Many times during this season of love's inquisition, the Lord would give me a vision of Jesus standing beside me and giving me a hug. On one occasion, I was worshiping the Lord, telling Him I loved Him, and He told me go outside and look up to the sky, for it was covered with tiny heart-shaped clouds. For fun, I sometimes ask for another example, and He never lets me down. Our relationship has grown into a sweet friendship, and I am amazed at how much fun we have together.

HEAVEN'S DEFINITION OF LOVE

What is Heaven's definition of love? I often find myself reading about Heaven's perfect example to remind me of how God feels about me. Reading First Corinthians 13 reminds us that heavenly love is God's heart toward us. Remember, as you read this, that if God is providing this as our example of how to love others, it is only because that is what He uses as His pattern and guideline to love us. He would never ask you to do something that He Himself is not capable of doing; therefore, when He requires us to love and forgive unconditionally, regardless of the circumstances, He sets the standard because it is the rule He Himself goes by.

A greater understanding about the love that the Lord has for us is explained in First John chapters 3 and 4. In First John 4:19 we learn that we love Him because He first loved us. What a comfort to know that no matter how badly we miss the mark He still loves and forgives us.

I would encourage you this day, if you struggle with questions of why or how God could love you, to ask the

Holy Spirit to show you how much God loves you. You, too, will be amazed at all the examples He will use to prove that you are valuable to Him in every way.

CHAPTER 10

BLESSING THOSE WHO CURSE YOU

Ah, the arduous task of forgiving...and forgiving... and forgiving. I had felt at times that it would have been easier to get a tooth pulled without Novocain than to forgive. Due to the depth of my traumas, I needed to be brought back to the place of forgiving numerous times, until every area of the oozing open sore was cleansed.

The Lord had been dealing with me repeatedly to forgive my ex-husband and the pastor and his wife who had falsely testified against me. Time after time, over months, the Lord would gently bring me back to the place of willingness and trust, to release them through forgiveness. After about six months of diligent work, I felt that I had been totally cleansed and that there was nothing left to forgive from my past.

I asked the Holy Spirit to reveal to me if there was any other area that I was holding onto. Instantly I had a vision, and in the spirit, He took me to a garden. As I looked around, I saw a big carrot whose root system extended deep into the ground. The Lord said this was a root of bitterness in my life. He told me to pull it up from the root and cast it into the sea, which I did.

Following that encounter, He instructed me to look up the pastor's church on the Internet and send the pastor an e-mail. I questioned if I had heard the Lord correctly for several days over it—while realizing any degree of disobedience with God was lawlessness—so I submitted and looked him up. God wanted to give me healing and restoration by the bushel and needed me to walk this path of forgiveness in order to prepare the way for the blessings He would pour out upon me. I successfully found the pastor's church Web site and sent him the following e-mail:

Dear Pastor,

It has been such a long time since we have spoken. I pray this letter finds you and your family in good health and happy. We have moved to Texas, and both my girls love it here and have adjusted well to all the changes....God has been so good to me these past five years. His grace and mercies surely are new every morning, and I am preparing to enter into ministry. I wanted to thank you for pastoring me for eight years. I learned many things under your tutelage. I also wanted to apologize for any offense between us. I do not understand how things got so difficult between us, and if I played any part in the matter, I ask you to forgive me. I look forward to visiting more with you in Paradise. Maybe one day I will run into you in the course of ministry, but until then, I pray blessings upon your family.

Sincerely,
Ronda Brown

He responded with the following e-mail:

Dear Ronda,

Thank you for your heartfelt letter. I know it was extremely difficult for both you and Jerry during those final years. When things go sour, couples often try to do their best from their perspective, and in the process, things simply deteriorate. What I know is this: Jerry has completed his course and is in a wonderful place, and I am blessed to know you and the girls are doing well. I hope only the best for you and your family.

God bless you always—
Pastor XXXX

P.S. In like manner, if I offended you in the difficult process we were all involved in, please forgive me. I forgive you.

Finally, I believed it was over for me. The bitterness was gone. The resentment and hatred relinquished. I was ready to move on and leave my past behind. But there was one more test the Lord required of me.

For one year, I had partnered and assisted with a local evangelist's ministry. I would help at his conferences as my schedule allowed. Just a few weeks following my e-mail exchange, I was scheduled to attend another of this friend's conferences. I was standing at the door as a greeter when the very pastor's wife (who had testified against me) and her middle daughter Suzie walked in. This conference was approximately four states away from their home. I had no idea how she even found out about the conference. My jaw hit the floor, and my heart began to race. It had been the first time I had come face-to-face or had spoken with her since the custody battle. I warmly greeted her with a clammy, shaking handshake—feeling my heart race, the blood actually pumping in my heart, and my face turn to scarlet. She was obviously overcome by our chance awkward meeting too and quickly left the room.

Falling into a heap of tears right there, I thought, *How could God have been so cruel? Why did He not warn me she was coming?* I had completely forgiven her—why then this agonizing test? Seeing her again immediately pulled me into the emotions of trauma, helplessness, and victimization; the memories were still as sharp, fearsome, and overwhelming as they ever were. But new fears surfaced as I realized I'd never broken completely free of those past false allegations and accusations. Very few in my new town knew of my history—a relocation across four state borders ensured that. I had friends now…ministry…a future. What if she spread more lies? What if her rumors infiltrated my life again? What if my ministry friend found out; what would he think? I wanted to run and hide—but I couldn't with the meeting just starting and with my volunteer duties.

As God would have it, He seated her directly in front of me—on the first row reserved for conference volunteers, pastors, and honored dignitaries. Actually she was in my usual seat. I couldn't concentrate on the service or on my duties. Rage reared its ugliness within me, and I kept telling the Lord, internally, how upset I was. The mountain grew as I thought of all of the painful work—the healing, the deliverances, mustering up the desire to even forgive her and her family—being all for naught, meaningless. Would her false allegations plague me all my life? Would I never be free from the stain of her accusatory shame?

All through worship and the sermon, my thoughts zeroed in on how they wronged me. How *their* testimony destroyed my life. How *their* testimony caused me to lose my youngest child for five years. How *their* testimony caused my daughters to experience deep emotional *and* physical scars. How *their* testimony caused an entire community to shun me.

God! I yelled out from the deepest place of my heart. *They ruined my life, and they sit here, unpunished, blessed, in fact. How could You allow this? Where is Your sense of judgment? Where is truth in all of this?* Oh, I forgave them I thought, but secretly I still expected them to be punished by God.

As clear as that day on the beach when I was about to kill myself, God spoke to me, though this time, in my spirit: *"Ronda, I will execute judgment on the entire family now if that is what you really want, but you will never see My glory or My presence again!"*

That's not fair...it's not fair, were my first thoughts. But then I recalled how for months I'd cried out to the Lord to see His glory, that I would dwell in His presence, that I would see Him face-to-face. Warm tears rolled down my cheeks to my chin to the floor. I wanted His glory more than anything else. I thought of her children—precious, innocent children. Everything within me knew God's full meaning and intent, and of course He was right! I knew what He meant and immediately sensed the seriousness of His proposition. Would I be "willing" to completely forgive this woman and man, whom God loved, or would I satisfy my own earthly revenge and choose to see their punishment—choose to see justice and God's vengeance lashing out at them.

Looking back on that time now, I know that the Lord meant it when He said that I would never see His glory again in this life or in life after death, for Scripture clearly shows that there is no personal forgiveness of our sin if we cannot forgive our offenders. Had I realized at that moment that my eternal sentence would be separation from the Lord, I may have been quicker to respond to Him.

It took only minutes to know that I hungered for His presence far more than I hungered for human justice. *"God, forgive me,"* I cried out. *"I release them into Your hands. Please forgive them. Please forgive me. Please bring **no** harm to them or their precious children."*

It was amazing how easily this prayer fell from my lips. But what happened next was a real test of the completeness of my deliverance from unforgiveness. Instantly the Lord took me into an open vision where I saw myself kneeling down at the woman's feet.

*"Oh, my God, this is **more** than I can bear. Please, my Lord, don't ask me to do this."* Even as I pled, obedience welled up within me until I was powerless to do anything else.

It Is Finished!

The evening service was about to close, and the final music was playing. Emotionally broken, I could no longer stand, but crawled on my knees from the end of the second row to the front row where she was seated. I saw her delicate foot, her beautifully painted toenails in attractive sandals. I knelt my face on the exposed part of her foot as tears dropped from my eyes and rolled over her toes. I do not know if she ever heard me as the music was loud, but I said, "Please forgive me for hating you." And in that instant I heard an *audible* voice from Heaven *shout* to my spirit, *"IT IS FINISHED!"* And with that I heard and saw tangible, metal stockade shackles unlock and fall hard to the ground from my ankles. With a loud clamor, metal hit the concrete below my feet; the sound was so very loud, I wondered if anyone else heard it.

It was over, and I knew it. I had been faithful to do all He had asked of me, and the moment I took those obedient steps, He released me from my history, from the shame that bound me to her accusations.

> *It is God that avengeth me, and subdueth the people under me. He delivereth me from mine enemies: yea, Thou liftest me up above those that rise up against me: Thou hast delivered me from the violent man* (Psalm 18:47-48).

From that day forward, greater increase and restoration began to manifest in my life. Doors of ministry started to open, and substantial finances flowed into my herbal Internet business. My intimacy with the Lord greatly increased from that day, as well as the tangible anointing I carried during altar ministry and prayer time. Routine prayers I prayed, God heard and answered.

God specifically began to use me in the area of emotional healing for wounded women in prisons and jails, and my prison ministry greatly increased from that point. Women were delivered, and the Lord seemed to touch and soften their hardened hearts, opening the door for salvation to manifest in their lives.

CHAPTER 11

KAIROS TIME

Supernatural connections and divine friendships formed for me. A holy hunger continued to rise up within my heart as I pressed deeper into the presence of the Lord. Quiet times in my bedroom blossomed into amazing visitations from the Lord. Angels made their presence known to me, and visions were routine. Once while I had been worshiping, the presence of Jesus walked into the room. He stood before me waving His arms above me, inhaling deeply my worship. He sat down in front of me and just looked at me. I was so amazed at His beauty. How often I had daydreamed about what I would say if I ever had this opportunity, but I found myself unable to say anything other than, *"You are so beautiful."*

Tears streamed down my face as my hand gently stroked the side of His cheek. I ran my hand across His hair, and as each strand danced through my fingers, the realness of His presence overwhelmed every emotion I had. I looked deeply into eyes that only said, "I love you." As He reached up and touched my face, I became extremely aware of His hands. Placing my hand over His, I gasped as my fingers felt His hand and the degree of His scars that He still carries. He simply cradled my face in His hand and smiled.

SUPERNATURAL BLESSINGS

My heart regularly sang with gratitude at all the Lord was doing in my life, and my lips were continually filled with praise as He routinely visited me. The Lord walked with me everywhere I went. One especially sweet day while driving to the store, I began thanking God for all He had done. Suddenly I was caught up in this glory cloud of high praise. I kept repeating and expressing to God, my passion for Him, "I bless You, God, I bless You," over and over.

 *I HAVE WAYS OF BLESSING YOU THAT YOU NEVER DREAMED OF, AND I BLESS YOU.*"

His presence was so strong in the car when He interrupted my praises in an audible voice: "Ronda, I bless you."

At first I was surprised at His comment. I thought, *Oh, that's sweet, Lord*, as if to minimize what He meant.

Then He said again, **"Ronda, I bless you,"** putting great emphasis on each word as if to give it priority. What He said next really caught my attention, actually surprising me. "Ronda, I have ways of blessing you that you never dreamed of, and I bless you."

124

Birthday Surprises

The words of the Lord that I'd received up until then, those words declared over me, were constantly being confirmed to me in visions. A month prior to my birthday, I began asking the Lord for a birthday present. It had become a sweet joke between us, and in case He forgot, I reminded Him daily that my birthday was coming and I wanted a birthday gift from Him. I asked Him for a "big, honkin' spiritual gift," not a tangible gift, and asked that He would wrap it in "pretty, pretty paper." Now I had no idea how He was going to wrap a spiritual gift in pretty, pretty paper, but I felt if He could create a universe, He could figure it out. Leaving Him with the details, I'd sing a song of reminder to Him and then laugh at how silly the little song sounded to me. Often I heard Him laugh at my silliness.

My birthday arrived, and so did a throbbing in my hand and arm, and then gold dust in the palm of my hands, particularly as I worshiped Him. It would appear just thinking about the Lord—that's all it took to get the golden glitter flowing. Concerned that there was something wrong with my arm, I asked the Lord what was happening. He reminded me of my birthday request and said that He gave me a healing anointing as a gift and that as the healing anointing flowed, so would the gold dust from my palms. And *that* was the pretty, pretty paper I asked for.

"I've wrapped your healing anointing in the gold dust," He said. Never a birthday goes by now that I don't remind the Father well in advance for a birthday gift. He's never disappointed me—He gives the most amazing gifts!

For this season of my life, I was under a supernatural canopy of God's unlimited grace that required only simple, child-like faith to activate.

THE BOOK TABLE ANOINTING

I had agreed to assist another evangelist friend who was holding a series of meetings. While at my duty station, the book table, I watched "Johnny" enter the room. Judging by the external smell and look, I perceived Johnny to be homeless. He quietly approached the book table accompanied by a female friend. After I greeted him, he shook his head and pointed to his friend. She immediately informed me that Johnny had been born without eardrums in his ears and had been unable to hear since his birth. Overcome with love, my heart ripped apart with grief for his loss. I stooped to get directly square with his face, eye-to-eye, and slowly mouthed for his permission to lay my hands on him for prayer. He nodded his head in agreement as I put my fingers inside the ear canals and prayed.

When we were done, and as he headed into the service, he screamed loudly, "I can hear! I can hear!" He jumped all over the place, praising God for the creative miracle of healing. I think I was more shocked than he was. Who knew how the innocence of a little prayer could exact such an incredible creative miracle!

In another meeting, again while I was at the book table, two men, both blind, asked me for prayer. As soon as I placed my hands over their eyes, my hands filled with gold dust, and their sight was restored. I call this my sweet time of innocence—for the love of God, I had been given the glory, as much as I wanted, and a little glimpse of things to come, without requirement on my end. I came to realize however, that as the Holy Spirit drew me ever closer into His presence, that miracle-working holiness does, in fact, come with a price.

Up until that point, life was good. Prison ministry was going well, bringing me abundant satisfaction, but there was more—much more—I knew there was more. The "more" was my deep desire to preach God's Word. Whole sermons formed in my mind. It was so frustrating to me to keep it all inside that I'd preach to the dog, to the mirror, to friends, over dinner—I'd target anyone and anything within earshot! I was faithful in my study of God's Word, and the Lord revealed deeper revelation. Insatiable hunger for His Word burned in the recesses of my deepest being. Glory!

PART III

RECOMPENSE

CHAPTER 12

THE SEA OF FORGETFULNESS

Eight years had passed since that initial experience with God on the beach. I had witnessed restoration in many areas of my life, and I was truly happy. I had been living in Texas for several years with my two daughters in a comfortable home in the country. My business was doing very well. I had been a prison chaplain for two years, and ministry was growing. Everything the enemy stole, the Lord powerfully restored sevenfold just as His Word promised.

A business meeting required that I return back to that same beach town for a short trip. It was June, and Lacie's birthday, so I offered to take her and treat her to a birthday excursion at Disney World. Upon arrival, I dropped her off with her friend and decided to drive my spiffy rented convertible out to the place where I had met the Lord some years ago. I looked forward to the opportunity to pray there again. My heart was so thankful for all He had done for me and in me.

I sat on the sand and quietly contemplated the many miracles wrought in my life. Tears pooled at my feet as my heart sang with gratitude for where I was and where He had brought me. Here He'd brought me full circle by my returning to the beach that day. Here I was sitting in the very same place where I'd found life and happiness truly for the first time.

"You know, Ronda, this is the eighth anniversary of the month that we met here," the Lord sweetly told me.

Yes, it was. I hadn't thought of the date before He said something. Then He showed that the number eight means "new beginnings," that this indeed was the place of my new beginnings. I rose from the sand and walked the shoreline, letting the cool water wash over my feet. A large stick lodged in the sand, and the Lord said, "Go ahead, pick it up, and use it as a staff," as He continued to speak to me.

SHAME

I headed with the staff toward a huge, man-made rock jetty that extended well past the tide break. As I walked its length, electricity coursed through my body, and I just knew the Lord had something planned. At the end of the quay, I rested on the rocks and leaned back against a small brick structure, anticipating His voice.

"Ronda, you wear shame like a red letter pinned to your chest."

Even though I had worked through complete forgiveness for those who hurt me, and the Lord had powerfully restored me, inwardly I still felt the shame of certain events; consequently, I still struggled with sharing those portions of my testimony in my preaching. My reputation, my name, and character had been so severely and viciously attacked by Jerry and unscrupulous people that I secretly still worried that someone would hear the lies and that my character would come under scrutiny again. Jerry's determination to label me an unfit, abusive mother or a crazy, paranoid woman was as a stench that never left my spirit.

THE SEA OF FORGETFULNESS

The Lord began speaking about a literal place called the *Sea of Forgetfulness*, where we can cast all pain and shame. "Today, I will do a new thing in your life," He said, "I will release a new and fresh power anointing for ministry." He said that He would part the sea and that I would walk through it on dry ground. No longer would I struggle, but things would come easier for me. He would take me into a new land that flowed with milk and honey, and then He spoke of ministry and of great things to come into my life.

"Stand up, stretch your staff over the sea," He said, and I did. In the spirit I heard the water part. It was very powerful. Then the Lord told me that there were those involved in the process of my divorce who had placed mantles of woundedness, shame, and accusation on my back, which I wore as a garment. "They are death rags and burial clothing," He said, "and they must be removed before I can lead you into the land I have for you." Then He instructed me to name aloud each garment as I removed them from my back.

"Reproach" was the first to go, and I actually made the motions to remove it like a jacket, while renouncing it.

"Throw it hard into the Sea of Forgetfulness, Ronda!"

Then He showed me the other layers I wore:

Betrayal

Victimization

Terror

Trauma

Torture

Imprisonment

Abuse

False Accusations

False Accusations of Child Abuse

False Accusations of Adultery

False Accusations of Being a Liar

False Accusations of Being an Unfit Mother

Shame

Each one, I peeled off and cast into the sea with force.

"Now, close the sea with your staff," He directed.

Trembling now as though I'd been hit by lightning, I extended my staff, closed the sea, and walked back to my car still shaking but feeling lighter—considerably lighter— with the lifting of those diabolical strongholds. I would never be the same again.

> *Who is a God like unto Thee, that pardoneth iniquity, and passeth by the transgression of the remnant of His heritage? He retaineth not His anger for ever, because He delighteth in mercy. He will turn again, He will have compassion upon us; He will subdue our iniquities; and* ***Thou wilt cast all their sins into the depths of the sea*** *(Micah 7:18-19).*

> *I have loved you with an everlasting love; therefore with loving-kindness have I drawn you and continued My faithfulness to you. Again I will build you and you will be built* (Jeremiah 31:3-4 AMP).

CHAPTER 13

KEYS TO RENEWAL

If you have suffered, or if you are suffering, the good news is this: you have made it thus far! So often I felt as though I couldn't take another bit without completely falling apart or coming undone. It sounds cliché, but it's truth: God promises never to give us more than we can bear. The exciting part about my life, and about yours, is that if you're going through challenges, *you did not die,* and He [God] who began a good work in you will be faithful to complete the work as long as you are willing to cooperate with the working of His Spirit and do your part. The Bible says, *"Be confident of this very thing...."* What very thing? The good work in you (see Phil. 1:6).

If I could share with you the major keys to my victory, it would be these:

1. Learn to be a worshiper, in the midst of your circumstances.

2. Learn to be a forgiver, in the midst of your circumstances.

As you do so, watch how quickly the Lord will turn things around for you to give you a hope and a future.

 *...WORSHIP WAS THE MAJOR KEY TO MY BREAKTHROUGH AND THE SIGNIFICANT REASON FOR MY RESTORATION.*

LEARN TO WORSHIP

I believe worship brought about the victory in every area of my life. Experiencing the realms of the supernatural became an everyday occurrence as I learned to worship the Lord my God. I remained victorious as long as I worshiped. During my recovery, I made worship my life's focus as I strove to worship the Lord 24/7 within my heart. As often as I could, I would get alone and sing His praises aloud, and I felt victorious, empowered, loved, and accepted. Worship took me to places I have never known were possible before. As I worshiped, I forgot about the pain and loss. I believe that worship was the major key to my breakthrough and the significant reason for my restoration.

King David in the Old Testament talks about having to stir himself up to worship. At times of heaviness when you are broken or fragmented, worship is the last thing on your mind. Depression feels like a heavy weight around your shoulders. Your victory comes when you force yourself to push past the pain and worship the Lord just because. Yes I had to engage in worship out of my pain and through difficult circumstances, most of the time worshiping without request or need, always mindful that He would be pleased in my praise.

Your praise will release a fresh oil of anointing upon you that will break every yoke, and your faith will pave the way for the situation to change. Worship is a form of warfare or intercession and accomplishes far more than you could ever imagine. Isaiah 61:3 actually talks about receiving a "garment" of praise over the spirit of despair or heaviness and depression. As you choose to worship the Lord even during times of heaviness and depression, your praise begins to cover and coat you and change the atmosphere around you to joy.

There are many ways to worship. Sometimes I sing along with a CD, or I get into a quiet place with a notebook and pen and listen as He speaks to me and then write down what He said. Sometimes I just lie down with everything off—no music, no worship, just silence—in the secret place of His presence. Whatever way we worship, as long as our minds remain on Him and His goodness, we're worshiping well.

FORGIVENESS IS POSSIBLE

My question was always, "How do I transition into the next step?" That might be your question too. It's a major one. Listen, I recognized that I had been the victim of horrible injustices. Those who harmed me needed forgiveness, and in my heart I was working toward that end, but how would I even begin to accomplish a task so major?

Only you can decide to move forward and walk away from your past hurts. I know this can be the most difficult step, and at the same time, the most empowering. We move forward by trusting and allowing the Holy Spirit to come and heal our deep wounds. Forgiving someone who has deeply wounded us does not mean that we are justifying their actions and thereby removing their guilt and accountability.

I learned that lesson the hard way. I thought that if I forgave them, they'd receive blessings instead of restitution. The fear that they wouldn't have to "pay" for their mistakes made me hesitate to openly forgive them. Someone had to pay, in my mind's eye, for the years of pain and loss the girls and I endured. The entire process of forgiveness seemed insurmountable, and yet I knew it was the will of the Father that I allow the Holy Spirit to begin to walk me through it.

FORGIVING SOMEONE WHO HAS DEEPLY WOUNDED US DOES NOT MEAN THAT WE ARE JUSTIFYING THEIR ACTIONS AND THEREBY REMOVING THEIR GUILT AND ACCOUNTABILITY.

I spent years trying to forget the most painful memories of my life and recalled only just enough to have a powerful testimony. I felt I resolved the majority of my pain through counseling, Christian inner healing, deliverance sessions, transparency, and accountability. But the Lord wanted to *completely* heal me from all the pain and the unbelievable loss that I *secretly* felt...those *hidden hurts* I was afraid to even look at, much less deal with…the stuff buried way deep down there in the innermost chambers of my heart.

Lacie (who herself now has a powerful testimony of the trauma she personally endured) once told me, "I know the Lord has purpose and destiny for me. I know He has a plan for my life, but working through my past in order to get to my future is more than I am strong enough to do." I related to this many times during my own healing process.

Once I made the conscious decision in my heart to begin to forgive those who hurt me, the job seemed massive. I had no idea where to begin. I started by praying that the Holy Spirit would soften my hardened heart toward those who hurt me and asked Him to bring me to a place to be able to forgive them. Every day I confessed audibly, "By an act of faith, I choose to forgive _____, regardless of my own personal woundedness." The pain was still so raw to me that for a while this was all I could pray.

Scripture says in Philippians 4:13 that we can do all things through Christ Jesus who strengthens us. Therefore, as I began my healing journey of forgiveness, in addition I confessed, "I can forgive _____ for _____ through Christ Jesus who strengthens me." This required a supernatural grace to even speak out of my mouth, and initially I spoke the words through gritted teeth. But it was only a very short time before my confession of faith caught up with my Spirit, and I was able to pray with more clarity and discernment over the hurt.

The Holy Spirit began to show me a plan of healing and restoration for myself that was easier to endure than I had originally thought. During that process, the Holy Spirit told me to begin to pray for them. I prayed general prayers at first, and out of them He would direct my prayer time revealing their specific needs.

Eventually, supernatural understanding and compassion replaced the hatred that often surfaced. I couldn't have mustered those things by my own strength. Once I could pray out of compassion, I knew that forgiveness toward them was taking root in my heart.

While this method may not be exact for everyone, it was the one way the Holy Spirit chose to begin the healing within me. I am sure that once you make your personal decision to forgive and ask the Holy Spirit to help you, He will give you a formula and the steps that will work perfectly for you.

Always remember, He desperately desires *for you to decide* to forgive and is anxiously waiting to come and heal your hurting heart and the situation when you ask Him to. In some cases, forgiveness may be needed for an organization or a body of people—for example, the justice system or the police department. These steps to forgiveness would also apply.

GOD'S JUSTICE WILL PREVAIL

My mom used to tell me not to worry about waiting to see justice prevail. Mixing Scripture and her own motherly advice, I can still hear her say, "Ronda girl, it is a fearful thing to fall into the hands of our living God. The wheels of justice grind slow, and they grind exceedingly fine, but you must forgive them."

King David spoke of this very thing in Psalm 73:2-19. David also noticed that at times it appeared that the wicked seem to prosper during their life. Justice and judgment appeared slow in coming to them.

For I was envious at the foolish, when I saw the prosperity of the wicked (Psalm 73:3).

But he continued, speaking of their demise:

*Surely Thou didst set them in slippery places: Thou castedst them down into destruction. How are they brought into desolation, as **in a moment!** They are utterly consumed with terrors* (Psalm 73:18-19).

As long as you remain in a position of passing judgment upon the person who caused you hurt or offense, you hinder the Lord's judging process. God is a God of justice and righteousness. He is a just Judge. God has a way of bringing restoration to us and judgment to them in ways we can't conceive of, but that must be left in the hands of God and the high court of Heaven alone.

For we know Him that hath said, Vengeance belongeth unto Me, I will recompense, saith the Lord. And again, The Lord shall judge His people. It is a fearful thing to fall into the hands of the living God (Hebrews 10:30-31).

Dearly beloved, avenge not yourselves, but rather give place unto wrath: for it is written, Vengeance is mine; I will repay, saith the Lord. Therefore if thine enemy hunger, feed him; if he thirst, give him drink:

for in so doing thou shalt heap coals of fire on his head. Be not overcome of evil, but overcome evil with good (Romans 12:19-21).

CHAPTER 14

FORGIVENESS: THE DNA
OF HEAVEN

Forgiveness is the key in maintaining the abundant blessings of God flowing in your life, and it is guaranteed to produce personal freedom and gigantic blessings in every area. Your ability to forgive is the key that unlocks every spiritual door. Forgiveness is the very DNA of Heaven. Forgiveness positions you to receive freely the fullness of Heaven. When you give yourself the gift of forgiveness, you free yourself to be all God called you to be.

The Lord knows your pain and the difficult time you have had in coming to this point. He saw everything that was done in secret against you. He heard their scheming plans. Nothing was hidden from His sight. He promises to bring reward and restoration in every area the enemy has stolen from you if you will trust Him and hand the painful memories over to Him. He will make the process much easier, and in the end you will have a twofold blessing. He will bring restoration to you in powerful ways, and you will have a powerful testimony that He will use for His Glory. Forgiveness is a win/win situation.

 *WHEN YOU GIVE YOURSELF THE GIFT OF FORGIVENESS, YOU FREE YOURSELF TO BE ALL GOD CALLED YOU TO BE.*

Thus saith the Lord, the God of David thy father, I have heard thy prayer, I have seen thy tears: behold, I will heal thee (2 Kings 20:5).

Forgiveness is a choice that comes with a wonderful surprise attached to it: restoration, in every area of your life… *Surprise!*…restoration in areas you never dreamed of and happiness beyond your wildest imagination!

FORGIVENESS IS PURE FAITH

God honors His Word. He honors faith. He honors obedience, and He rewards your obedience! When you choose to obey His Word, He delights in showering you with blessings! Forgiveness is faith in action. It is trusting that God will make a way for you and will not allow the offense against you to go unpunished. Forgiveness is placing your faith upon the Word of God and believing that He will pick up your cause and judge your case rightly and fairly. Therefore, forgiveness is genuine faith in its purest form.

146

It takes a great act of faith to be willing to come before God and release the one who caused you so much pain. God always rewards that measure of faith. Yes, God honors faith. He said He is pleased through our faith (see Heb. 11:6). God honors forgiveness. He will honor your willing heart and each step you take toward handing the hurts over to Him.

What does forgiveness look like? No longer are your eyes focused upon the offender or the circumstances surrounding the painful event, but as you begin to shift over to God's way of thinking, a supernatural grace for your healing is released in your life. Powerfully the Lord begins to cauterize the open gashes of your heart.

WHAT DOES GOD'S WORD SAY ABOUT FORGIVENESS?

Forgiveness empowers the Word of God to act on your behalf. In the New Testament, the word *forgive* (as found in Luke 6:37) is *apoluo;* which means to free fully, or to relieve, release, dismiss, let die, or pardon. It also means to let go, loose, send away, and set at liberty.[1]

Judge not, and ye shall not be judged: condemn not, and ye shall not be condemned: forgive, and ye shall be forgiven (Luke 6:37).

Webster's dictionary defines *forgive* as

1. To give up all claims.

2. To cease to feel resentment against (an offender).

3. To cancel any liability.

4. To pardon an offense or offender.[2]

The word *restore* is used 40 times in the Bible, and that's not surprising since it's God's heart to restore His people. The number *40* is biblically significant because it is the number for tests and trials (for example, the Israelites wandered in the desert for 40 years. In the days of Noah, it rained for 40 days and 40 nights. Jesus fasted for 40 days).

Webster's dictionary defines *restore* as

1. To put or bring back into existence or use.

2. To bring back or put back into a former or original state: renew.

3. To give back or return.[3]

The word *restore* in the Bible also means "to recompense, recover, refresh, relieve, render, requite, rescue, retrieve, (cause to, make to) return, reverse, reward."[4]

And I will restore to you the years that the locust hath eaten, the cankerworm, and the caterpillar, and the palmerworm, my great army which I sent among you. And ye shall eat in plenty, and be satisfied, and praise the name of the Lord your God, that hath dealt wondrously with you... (Joel 2:25-26).

Therefore all they that devour thee shall be devoured; and all thine adversaries, every one of them, shall go into captivity; and they that spoil thee shall be a spoil, and all that prey upon thee will I give for a prey. **For I will** *restore health unto thee, and I will heal thee of thy wounds, saith the Lord; because they called thee an Outcast* (Jeremiah 30:16-17).

*Behold, at that time **I will deal with all who afflict you;** I will save the lame, and gather those who were driven out; I will appoint them for praise and fame in every land where they were put to shame* (Zephaniah 3:19 NKJV).

He that toucheth you toucheth the apple of His eye (Zechariah 2:8).

When you decide to set your mind, will, and emotions toward forgiving that one who hurt you, the Holy Spirit gently moves you through the steps necessary for your own total healing and restoration. A job that initially seemed insurmountable becomes much easier because the Lord wants you healed and restored faster than you do! And all He needed was your willing heart to begin the process.

Question: How many times a day do you have to forgive someone?

Answer: As many times as it takes!

In my case, it was not just once but often once every day as the enemy would replay the offense over and over in my head. Having to forgive someone continually does not discredit your original action. It simply means that you are on the right track and that your heart is completely open and willing to forgive. You just keep confessing that you forgive and keep asking the Holy Spirit to do His part in your heart, and total forgiveness will eventually manifest for you.

Then came Peter to Him, and said, Lord, how oft shall my brother sin against me, and I forgive him? till seven times? Jesus saith unto him, I say not unto thee, until seven times: but, until seventy times seven (Matthew 18:21-22).

BITTERNESS

Through your act of forgiveness, you personally *choose* to release *all* your bitterness. Bitterness is like a poison that becomes rooted in the heart, simply because you do not understand the biblical meaning of Christ-like forgiveness. Before long, Christ-like fruit in your own personal garden is replaced by huge carrots of bitterness, whose root system grows deep under the surface.[5] Unchecked, bitterness has a way of taking on a life of its own. *Uncontrolled* bitterness can spread and infect every area of life, poisoning every relationship you hold as valuable. Through your anger and bitterness, the offender continues to maintain a sense of power and control over your life.

The Bible defines *bitterness* as a "poison."[6] Webster's dictionary defines *bitterness* as "resentful; characterized by intense hostility; caused by pain."[7] Bitterness is said to be like the act of personally drinking poison and hoping that the other person dies. Only you can make the choice to release your bitterness and all desires for secret retaliation—including all secret desires to see, hear, or witness their punishment—when you choose to forgive. Bitterness only eats at you as you sit and wait (and wait and wait) for your vengeance. Bitterness actually imprisons you in your own negativity. In addition, bitterness and unforgiveness make hearing the voice of the Holy Spirit very difficult. Bitterness can even be the root of disease—real, physical illness.

It is the nature of man to return evil for evil and retaliate with hatred or ugly, unkind words, but someone who has a heart for God will choose to follow His Word and the way of the cross, which strictly commands us to forgive those who hurt us.

Francis Frangipane, in his teaching *Bitterness in the Garden of Our Hearts,* wrote, "A bitter soul is a spirit trapped in a time warp...they live in the memory of their pain."[8]

Unforgiveness and bitterness retain the sins of your past, bringing them into your present state; and if left untreated, they will affect your future and every relationship with others. Ask the Lord to change your way of thinking by being slow to take an offense and refusing to accept hurt feelings through bitterness.[9]

THE CHARACTERISTICS OF BITTERNESS

- A bitter person cares very little for the person he is bitter against.

- He is very touchy.

- He can be ungrateful.

- He gives empty flattery and harsh criticism.

- He holds grudges and finds it difficult to forgive.

- He displays stubbornness or a sulky attitude.

- He will help no one or complains sometimes when asked to help.

- He experiences mood extremes—highs and lows.[10]

STAGES OF BITTERNESS

Here are the typical stages of bitterness:

- Oversensitivity to a verbal remark, action, or lack of action.

- Hurt feelings.

- Repulsive feelings toward a person at the thought or sight of them.

- Retaining wounds and frequently talking about them.

- Alienation of a person.

- Verbal slander against the person.

- Lack of obedience.

- Becoming like the one you despise.[11]

Through bitterness, you remain trapped and locked in the valley of brokenness. Unforgiveness prevents you from leaving. In the valley of brokenness bitterness weaves its way through your DNA and into every part of your life. Body, soul, and spirit all begin to experience brokenness and eventually shut down, from which the only escape is a willingness to forgive. Forgiveness aligns you with the will of God, which shifts you from the valley of brokenness to the mountain of restoration.

No matter what positive or negative method you attempt to use to ease your pain and mend your broken heart, without genuine forgiveness the underlying condition will fail to bring about permanent healing and will manifest in a variety of other symptoms such as: depression, sickness, sleep disorders, disease, OCD (Obsessive Compulsive Disorder), eating disorders, or a tendency toward an overbearing and controlling nature.

> *Follow peace with all men, and holiness, without which no man shall see the Lord: Looking diligently lest any man fail of the grace of God; lest any root of bitterness springing up trouble you, and thereby many be defiled* (Hebrews 12:14-15).

> *Let all bitterness, and wrath, and anger, and clamor, and evil speaking, be put away from you, with all malice: And be ye kind one to another, tenderhearted, forgiving one another, even as God for Christ's sake hath forgiven you* (Ephesians 4:31-32).

> *Repay no one evil for evil* (Romans 12:17 NKJV).

HEALING ROOMS

When severe woundedness is present, complete forgiveness as well as inner healing may require some additional assistance.

In cases of extreme woundedness or severe abuse, you may need to pursue a more structured approach of inner healing with loving Christian people who are trained and familiar with similar hurts and issues.

There is no shame or failure on your part in contacting someone who can lovingly guide and encourage you through the complete healing process. We all desire the same results, that you will be whole and happy, experiencing life in every area of your body, mind, soul, and spirit.

Some programs I recommend are "Restoring the Foundations" or "Cleansing Streams." I also like the complete structured program offered through the "Elijah House." Many Charismatic churches today offer qualified inner healing programs to anyone who is interested. Healing Rooms are also wonderful tools for any degree of woundedness.

To locate a healing room close to you, visit International Association of Healing Rooms (IAHR) at www.healingrooms .com or call (509) 456-0517. Though IAHR does not offer any type of counseling, they are a wonderful resource for prayer.

At this point, I do believe that if your heart has been touched toward the possibility to forgive, the Holy Spirit is dealing with you and therefore wants to release every tool necessary for you to accomplish complete forgiveness. Regardless of the horrible offense and the damage that was done, Jesus has the power, the grace, and the desire to supernaturally empower every tool for you to forgive and release them.

FORGIVENESS IS A CHOICE

Forgiveness is not a feeling, but rather a personal choice. When you can separate your feelings from your choices, the process becomes easier. Forgiveness takes place right where you are while emotionally broken, bloody, and bruised. Only the Holy Spirit can effectively heal your feelings. Forgiveness is your obedient choice to follow the example of Jesus and His command to release your bitterness and offense.

FORGIVENESS IS NOT A FEELING, BUT RATHER A PERSONAL CHOICE.

In most cases, forgiveness does not occur face-to-face with your offender. Forgiveness is simply emotional and mental housecleaning—a mental shift or adjustment in our thinking, one that says we no longer desire personal revenge but are willing to embrace the way of the cross.[12]

Forgiveness shifts our requirement for their payment or penalties from our responsibility to God's responsibility. Truthfully we do not have the ability to actually require anyone's penalty for their wrong actions. Somehow we reason that we might, but in actuality there is nothing we can do to render their true repentance or judgment.

Forgiveness frees you from mentally enforcing or requiring judgments. Through forgiveness you agree to the mental canceling of any debt owed. God has a way of judging an unrepentant heart far better than you do. He has ways of exacting penalties beyond your imagination. It is time to let

God handle the God stuff and let us handle the stuff He gave to us.

God has given everyone the ability to make choices. Every day presents new choices to us. In each choice, we can choose to live by God's standards or by man's lawlessness. Forgiveness is being willing to lay down your own hurts (including those that resulted from **unjustified** wrongs) in order to be obedient to the Word of God, which states that He requires forgiveness in every situation and He offers wholeness as our exchange. Heaven greatly rewards such obedience!

In Acts 6-7, we read about Stephen's amazing testimony of forgiveness in the face of his death. Stephen was appointed by the apostles to oversee the widows' ministry. The Bible said in verse 8 that Stephen was full of faith and power and that he did great wonders and miracles among the people. The Jewish priests felt threatened and schemed to have him arrested. Stephen, full of the Holy Spirit, recited a magnificent account of the historical events that prophesied the coming life and crucifixion of Jesus. At his conclusion, the priests dragged him out to be stoned. While suffering Stephen prayed, "*'Lord Jesus, receive my spirit.' And he kneeled down, and cried with a loud voice, 'Lord, lay not this sin to their charge.' And when he had said this, he fell asleep*" [meaning he died] (Acts 7:59-60).

Likewise, Jesus, upon His own death, prayed a similar prayer in Luke 23:34, "*...forgive them; for they know not what they do.*"

Learning to forgive *is* learning to think and act as the Word of God requires us to. This is when you have to trust that God sees, knows, and makes all things right, just as He promised He would. Jesus wants us as free as He died to make us.

Once your heart has chosen to forgive, your choice releases a fresh wave of the Lord's grace to carry you through the task. With knowledge comes power, and when you understand the reason why you forgive, you will be empowered with the ability to forgive through the power and strength of the Holy Spirit.

THE MANY BENEFITS AND PURPOSE OF FORGIVENESS ARE PRIMARILY FOR YOU AND NOT FOR THE OFFENDER.

TWO LITTLE WORDS

"I'm sorry" are the two little words that we all would like to hear and yet rarely do. Wouldn't an apology make things so much easier? In so many cases where true forgiveness is necessary, it is because an apology or explanation was never offered. Requiring an apology for wrong actions or behavior is not the basis for forgiveness or the purpose of forgiveness. You may be waiting forever if you expect an apology in order to be able to release forgiveness to your offender. Forgiveness is more a gift you give yourself; the results bring you peace, wholeness, happiness, healing, and restoration. The many benefits and purpose of forgiveness are primarily for you and not for the offender.

UNFORGIVENESS HINDERS OUR PRAYER LIFE

Many people today don't consider unforgiveness to be among the "major sins" (like murder or adultery). However, did you know that it is one of the main hindrances why the Lord doesn't answer our personal prayers? Our prayers can be hindered if we harbor any degree of unforgiveness, which the Word of God declares is sin. The resulting sin (of unforgiveness) is referred to as a brass or bronze heaven in Deuteronomy 28:23.

Think about offenses and unforgiveness like this: Say you are out in your yard, watering your garden, and you get a kink in the hose. The water stops flowing. If you don't water your flowers, eventually they will die. Available to you are 10 million gallons of water sitting in a water tower somewhere, but one little twist, one little kink in the hose, stops it from flowing to its needed destination. You have all of God's power available to you, but unforgiveness can be just the thing that stops it from flowing in your life. It is so important that we get free of all unforgiveness, bitterness, strife, or offense to keep the river of God free flowing at all times. We are reminded in Proverbs 4:23 that out of the heart flow the issues of life. Guard your heart and keep it with all diligence.[13]

You have all of God's power available to you, but unforgiveness can be just the thing that stops it from flowing in your life.

If I regard iniquity in my heart, the Lord will not hear me (Psalm 66:18).

Behold the Lord's hand is not shortened, that it cannot save; nor His ear heavy, that it cannot hear. But your iniquities have separated you from your God; and your sins have hidden His face from you, so that He will not hear (Isaiah 59:1-2 NKJV).

...Your sins have withheld good from you (Jeremiah 5:25 NKJV).

So your question needs to be, when Jesus looks at you, does He see Himself in you? When you forgive, you are acting in obedience to both the Word and the will of Jesus. Your identity is transformed into His identity. When He looks at you, He sees Himself in and through you.

THE PRIDE OF UNFORGIVENESS

The reason unforgiveness is so serious is that it is a form of pride. God as Creator humbled Himself in and through Jesus and paid the penalty for our death and sin on the cross. Since God forgave us, He requires us to forgive others, and it is considered sin and lawlessness according to First John 3:4 when we do not forgive those who offend us. By not forgiving them and instead insisting on their punishment, we are essentially judging them. Since only Jesus is qualified to judge sin, holding unforgiveness is direct disobedience to God's Word, which requires us to forgive—and is, therefore, sin.

ENDNOTES

1. "Apoluo;" http://www.studylight.org/lex/grk/view.cgi?number=630.

2. *Merriam-Webster's Collegiate Dictionary*, 11th ed., s.v. "Forgive."

3. *Merriam-Webster's Collegiate Dictionary*, 11th ed., s.v. "Restore."

4. "Shalam"; http://www.studylight.org/lex/heb/view.cgi? number =07999

5. See http://www.openheaven.com/forums/forumposts.asp?TID =9616&PN=1 (accessed June 8, 2009).

6. "Ro'sh"; http://www.studylight.org/lex/heb/view.cgi?number =07219

7. *Merriam-Webster's Collegiate Dictionary*, 11th ed., s.v. "Bitterness."

8. See Francis Frangipane's article at http://www.icitc.org/cgi-bin/ gx.cgi/AppLogic+FTContentServerpagename=FaithHighway/Globals/ DisplayTextMessage&PROJECTPATH= 10000/1000/728&sermonid =textsermon_ 1171590895619&customerTypeLabel=Weekly&sermont itle=Deliverance%20From%20Bitterness.

9. See http://upstreamca.org/bitterness.html (accessed February 15, 2009).

10. This table was taken from http://upstreamca.org/bitterness .html (accessed February 15, 2009). Used by permission.

11. This list of stages appears in the article, "Bitterness and Unforgiveness;" http://prophecyfellowship.yuku.com/topic/6578/ t/Bitterness-and-Unforgiveness.html (accessed May 16, 2009).

12. See http://www.iloveulove.com/downloads/Forgiveness% 20&%20Health%202001.pdf (accessed June 8, 2009).

13. The water hose illustration and other ideas in this paragraph were gleaned from "Unforgiveness Is Disobedience;" http://www .24-hour-prayer.org/unforgiveness.html (accessed May 16, 2009).

CHAPTER 15

FROM VICTIM TO VICTOR

By laying down every desire you have for your offender's punishment and allowing the Lord to deal with them, you transform your self-identity. In so doing, you no longer remain the victim. Your victory is absolutely guaranteed. By being willing to trust the Word of the Lord and His judging system, you have now positioned yourself directly *beside* God who has free access to heal you *and* turn the situation in your favor.

Forgiveness releases all ungodly mindsets that require someone to pay for the pain you suffered and replaces them with the assurance that God, who sees all those things done in secret, will rightly judge and render a verdict based upon His high court, His own judicial system, and in His timing. Once God issues a verdict, God's judgments are strong, swift, and serious. (Yikes! I wouldn't want to be on that side of consequence.)

Be not deceived; God is not mocked: for whatsoever a man soweth, that shall he also reap. For he that soweth to his flesh shall of the flesh reap corruption; but he that soweth to the Spirit shall of the Spirit reap life everlasting (Galatians 6:7-8).

Jesus alone is allowed legal permission to judge sin and release penalties. Jesus forgives us, and we forgive others. As we forgive others, He forgives us. Jesus set us free from all the penalties of our own sin, and this is to be our only model for anyone who has wronged or hurt us.

God never intended for you to forget your pain as a part of your own healing. Forgiving is *not* forgetting; but rather, forgiving is releasing so that healing can take place in you. Through the love of Jesus and the work of the Holy Spirit, He offers to take it, heal you, and use it for your good and His glory. Wow, what a win/win concept!

FORGIVING IS NOT FORGETTING; BUT RATHER, FORGIVING IS RELEASING SO THAT HEALING CAN TAKE PLACE IN YOU.

FORGIVENESS DOES NOT EXCUSE

Once you understand that through your choice of forgiveness, the offender or wrong action is not excused and released by the Father (the minute you choose to forgive), it will make the process much easier. Forgiveness does not make excuses for the hurtful action and the resulting pain and trauma that followed. It in no way minimizes what you endured and how that pain affected or changed your life. Forgiveness does not mean you deny the offender's responsibility. It means you choose to release the pain you suffered and leave the consequences to the Lord.

> *Dearly beloved, avenge not yourselves, but rather give place unto wrath: for it is written, Vengeance is Mine; I will repay, saith the Lord. Therefore if thine enemy hunger, feed him; if he thirst, give him drink: for in so doing thou shalt heap coals of fire on his head. Be not overcome of evil, but overcome evil with good* (Romans 12:19-21).

I like the way the Living Bible puts it:

> *Never avenge yourselves. Leave that to God, for He has said that He will repay those who deserve it. [Don't take the law into your own hands.] Instead, feed your enemy if he is hungry. If he is thirsty give him something to drink and you will be "heaping coals of fire on his head." In other words, he will feel ashamed of himself for what he has done to you. Don't let evil get the upper hand, but conquer evil by doing good* (Romans 12:19-21 TLB).

Your forgiveness in no way releases those who wronged you from being required to both pay and reap a harvest of destruction from the curse they have brought upon their own life.

> *The curse of the Lord is in the house of the wicked* (Proverbs 3:33).

For the Lord loves justice, and does not forsake His saints; they are preserved forever, but the descendants of the wicked shall be cut off (Psalm 37:28 NKJV).

There are no qualifying conditions that would exclude you from forgiving under "certain" situations. The laws of God are clear that we are not to hate, slander, gossip, backbite, grumble, seek revenge, or desire punishment against anyone. I am quite sure that when the Holy Spirit wrote this He completely knew and understood that people would hurt and turn on each other, including and especially their own family members. Regardless of the details, in every situation Jesus commanded us to forgive.

Whoever hates his brother is a murderer, and you know that no murderer has eternal life abiding in him (1 John 3:15 NKJV).

Anyone who says he is walking in the light of Christ but dislikes his fellow man is still in darkness. But whoever loves his fellow man is "walking in the light" and can see his way without stumbling around in darkness and sin. For he who dislikes his brother is wandering in spiritual darkness and doesn't know where he is going, for the darkness has made him blind so that he cannot see the way (1 John 2:9-11 TLB).

WHEN THEY FALL

In Proverbs 24:17-18 the Lord specifically warns us not to rejoice when judgment begins against our enemy. This command carries a direct promise or warning. If you continue to rejoice either secretly or outwardly, the Lord will see it and stop the judgment against them.

> *Do not rejoice when your enemy falls, and do not let your heart be glad when he stumbles; lest the Lord see it, and it displease Him, and He turn away His wrath from him* (Proverbs 24:17-18 NKJV).

I experienced this firsthand. During my divorce Jerry had a stroke, which grotesquely paralyzed half of his face. Just the pitiful sight of his dragging, drawn face sent waves of joy over me. *Vengeance*, I thought, as I laughed aloud each time we passed in the court halls. The doctors told him they were unsure if the paralysis would ever improve. My revenge and great delight in his demise was short-lived, however, because before long he "miraculously" improved, and his facial muscles completely returned to normal.

We are warned to both love and forgive our enemies, thus heaping coals of fire upon their heads. When we rejoice in their punishment, however, we halt the judgment of God. Again it comes back to the question of who will be judge, you or God. God will not allow both the privilege. Since we do not have a legal right to judge and our judgment produces nothing except curses upon our heads, isn't that a job best left to God?

> *He who is glad at calamity will not go unpunished* (Proverbs 17:5b NKJV).

FORGIVENESS MEANS THAT YOU TOO ARE FORGIVEN

Basic biblical fact: forgive, and you shall be forgiven. By forgiving you align yourself with both the will and the Word of God, and He, in turn, offers you full forgiveness and complete pardon as an exchange.

There have been so many times that I have royally messed up, but I had the deep assurance in my heart that with each transgression I committed, I was totally and instantly forgiven because I repented—and on the basis that I am willing to forgive others, regardless of the offense. Now this is by no means a license to sin. As godly men and women, our lives need daily to be an example of holiness and godliness, but we do unintentionally blow it at times. And let me tell you, the fact that I am willing to be a quick forgiver brings about a deep peace within my heart when I personally sin and require forgiveness myself. Once I learned this principle, the enemy lost a great foothold in his attempts to bring condemnation against me. Because I forgive others when I personally repent, I am instantly forgiven, and there is no longer any room for condemnation against me.

The enemy's condemnation is very different from the loving conviction the Holy Spirit offers. The Holy Spirit's conviction is always precise and direct. For example, if you treated your mother poorly, the Holy Spirit might say that you need to repent to her regarding the specific incident and ask for her forgiveness. When the enemy condemns and brings shame, it is very general and targets who you are as a whole, instead of what you did. Using the same example, the enemy would say you are a horrible person and therefore not worthy of forgiveness. You don't even deserve a mother at all. You are going to be a horrible mother yourself.

The enemy may have a legal right continually to bring condemnation against you through your own unforgiveness. If the enemy repeatedly tells you that your own sin is too great for the Lord to forgive, or he persistently reminds you of what a sinner or total loser you are, check your own heart. Then ask the Holy Spirit to reveal if you are holding unforgiveness against someone, as that may in itself be enough ground for him to have an open door into your life to accuse you.

IN FORGIVING ANOTHER, WE AGREE TO STOP DWELLING ON OR REPLAYING THE OFFENSE IN OUR MIND.

MEMORY EXCHANGE

Forgiveness requires your mental determination. In forgiving another, we agree to stop dwelling on or replaying the offense in our mind. This was the hardest area for me to overcome. With my mouth I would confess that I forgave, and in my heart I believed that I desired to forgive; however, I could not get the painful images out of my mind. They bombarded me constantly. The enemy played them again and again in an effort to keep me worn down emotionally and to keep me bound to bitterness. I would cry out for the images to stop, but they never would.

In the spirit realm, the more I thought about them, the more I gave them a legal access to be there, thus imprisoning my own mind. I was trapped in a vicious cycle I did not know how to end.

In addition, unforgiveness gives the enemy legal ground to release a spirit of torment into our mind.

When I asked the Holy Spirit to help me, He gave me a key that in my case was extremely successful. This key may not be the key that works for you, but I know that if you ask Him to, He will give you a key that will work. For me, He took me to Philippians 4:8:

> *Finally, brethren, whatever things are true, whatever things are noble, whatever things are just, whatever things are pure, whatever things are lovely, whatever things are of good report, if there is any virtue and if there is anything praiseworthy—meditate on these things* (Philippians 4:8 NKJV).

I wrote the verse out and carried it around to memorize. Every time one of those awful images entered, I would begin to recite the verse by memory. I usually had to laugh because I always mixed up the words, but I tried so hard to recite the verse that the offense vanished. It was not long before the images stopped altogether and I was experiencing freedom in every area that before had only brought mental distress and great secret pain.

When you apply a Bible verse as a memory exchange, you must be extremely diligent initially to catch each thought immediately and not allow it to run repeatedly in your mind. According to Second Timothy 1:7 the Word declares that you have the mind of Christ and that God has not given you a spirit of fear but of power, love, and a sound mind (see also 1 Cor. 2:16). You will not lose your mind! You are not close to losing you mind; the enemy is a liar. Your mind is sound.

By applying a Bible verse as a memory exchange, you will be amazed at how quickly you will regain control over your mind and stop every hurtful, tormenting memory. It is time to take back what belongs to you (your mind) and use it for the glory of God.

> *Brethren, I count not myself to have apprehended: but this one thing I do, forgetting those things which are behind, and reaching forth unto those things which are before, I press toward the mark for the prize of the high calling of God in Christ Jesus* (Philippians 3:13-14).

SPIRITUAL RE-EVALUATION

Another great healing tool the Holy Spirit showed me was to take each painful memory individually before the Father and ask for an exchange in the spirit. I call this the *Spiritual Re-Evaluation*. He taught me to ask Him to show me the painful memory through His eyes instead of mine. This "paradigm" shift helps you to see things in a way you never saw before. I have used this technique many times with each plaguing memory.

One hard memory for me was back before Jerry and I separated. It was late one night. Jerry entered our bedroom, jumped on top of me, pinning my arms down under the weight of his knees and with both hands around my neck tried to strangle me as I lay helpless in my bed. I felt like any second I would die. I was so afraid. However, suddenly he stopped with no explanation and walked out of the room. Sadly, afterward, I questioned God's lack of protection for me during that attack. During my healing process after I handed the painful memory over to Jesus, I asked Him to show me the truth behind that evening and why He didn't come to my aid. Jesus took me into a vision, and I saw Jerry's murderous hands around my throat choking the breath from me. Then I saw something I never knew. Just under Jerry's hands were Jesus' hands. Jesus was holding Jerry's hands. Jesus told me that on that evening, Jerry *had* intended in his heart to kill me, but that He, Jesus, was there all the time preventing it. Seeing that painful memory through the eyes of Jesus brought instant healing. Not only did the memory never bother me again, but also pain was exchanged for thanksgiving that the Lord spared my life (yet again).

I have used that same prayer often with other painful experiences, asking the Holy Spirit to show me the event through His eyes, and it has changed my perspective and memory of the painful time. This is the basic prayer I have used:

Dear Jesus

My heart hurts when I think about _____. Will You please show me this memory through Your eyes? I ask Your Holy Spirit to begin to heal me, body, soul, and spirit from this memory, to heal the pain, remove the hurtful memory, and the negative emotion attached to this memory. I ask You to heal every part of me that was wounded, damaged, or splintered. I choose to no longer dwell on the pain of this memory. I release this memory and its pain to You now, and I ask You for an exchange in the spirit and for Your restoration in this area. Amen.

As you ask Jesus to show you the memory through His eyes, the results can be freeing and healing. Jesus is anxious to bring healing to you in every area. If you get quiet and ask Him to reveal truth to you regarding the painful memory, this can be a very effective healing tool. Trust that in His goodness and love for you, He won't reveal anything that you can't bear. What God reveals, God heals!

FORGIVENESS DETERMINES DESTINY

When you step into the mind of Christ and His way of thinking, you operate under the full ability to succeed in every area of your life. Forgiveness opens up Heaven for you and makes the impossible possible.

I am convinced that when we hold unforgiveness against others we are shackled to them. Not only will they be judged for their offense, but we'll be equally judged for our unforgiveness.

Our own ability to forgive determines where we will spend eternity! Once again, the choice is yours. The Word of God is extremely clear about this. If we cannot forgive, then neither will we be forgiven. *God is not mocked; whatsoever a man sows that shall he also reap* (see Gal. 6:7). If we sow unforgiveness, then that is what we will be shown.

If we could see that holding onto the offense and the unforgiveness *will* hinder us from going to Heaven and may well send us to hell, we may be a little quicker to forgive and allow God to deal with our offender as He sees fit.

Judge not, and ye shall not be judged: condemn not, and ye shall not be condemned: forgive, and ye shall be forgiven (Luke 6:37).

If you are still not convinced, consider Matthew 6:15. Jesus could not state this any clearer. If you do not forgive others, you are not allowed into the Kingdom of Heaven:

But if ye forgive not men their trespasses, neither will your Father forgive your trespasses (Matthew 6:15).

CHAPTER 16

THE PRICE OF UNFORGIVENESS

In her book, *A Divine Revelation of Hell,*[1] Mary K. Baxter gives her account of being taken into hell by the Lord and shown many people who refused to forgive. Below are excerpts of one testimony of the penalty of unforgiveness.

> All along the pathway of hell burning hands reached out to Jesus from pits. Jesus stopped at one pit and said, "I called this woman to preach My Word for many years, and she grew in the knowledge of the Lord. She learned My voice, studied the Word of God, prayed often, and had many prayers answered. She was faithful in her house.
>
> One day she found out that her husband was having an affair with another woman. And even though he asked for forgiveness, she *grew bitter and would not*

forgive him or try to save her marriage. True, her husband was wrong, and he did commit a very grave sin. But this woman knew My Word. *She knew to forgive.* Her husband asked her to forgive him. She would not. Instead, anger took root and grew inside her. She would not turn it over to Me. She turned more bitter each day. He came to her and repented and said he would never do that again. "Lord," she said, "I am the holy one, and he is the sinful one." She would not listen to Me. Her heart grew bitter, and great sin entered in. I listened as she responded to Jesus. "I will forgive now, Lord," she said. "Let me out. I will obey You now."

THE RESURRECTION OF REV. DANIEL EKECHUKWU[2]

Here is another account of the seriousness of unforgiveness and its eternal consequences, as told by David Servant.

Reverend Daniel Ekechukwu died on the night of November 30, 2001, and was raised from the dead on December 2, 2001, during which time the Lord showed him both Heaven and Hell.

On Thursday, November 29th, 2001, Pastor Daniel Ekechukwu and his wife Nneka had a argument that ended in her slapping him. He was very offended by this incident, to the point of not even acknowledging her attempt to reconcile the next morning. Pastor Daniel admitted that throughout the day of November 30th, he angrily thought about how he would put his wife in her place when he returned home.

Nneka had begged Daniel to forgive her for slapping him, but he had refused. He said such a thing (a wife slapping a husband) is never done in his country [Africa]. It is an "abomination." His intention was to wait until after church on Sunday and to ban her for one year's separation from him to his father's compound in the village.

He was driving home that evening when the brakes on his car failed as he was heading down a steep hill. His car crashed into a concrete pillar. Daniel knew he was dying and began asking God to forgive him of all his sins so that he would be ready to stand before the Lord. He sent for his wife Nneka with whom he had refused to speak when he left his home earlier that day. He began to give her instructions about certain church and personal documents, and admonishing her to take care of their sons and his church.

Daniel saw two large angels as they lifted him from either side. Once in Paradise Daniel stood with the angel and watched a multitude of worshipping people who were dressed in sparkling white garments. Daniel longed to join the worshippers, but the angels told him that there were other things Daniel needed to see.

Next they showed him the mansions Jesus has prepared for His children. Daniel said there is no earthly way to describe what he saw. Daniel heard beautiful singing. Wondering where the music was coming from, the angel immediately pointed him to the many flowers around the mansion. When Daniel looked at them more closely, they were moving and swaying and singing praise to God!

Next the angel took Daniel to Hell, and they stood at the gates of Hell. When the angel lifted his hand and let it fall again, the gate opened, and Daniel could immediately hear the awful sounds of people screaming and weeping, but everything in hell was in total blackness. Then a bright light shone from the angel, and Daniel could see many groups of people in anguish.

The escorting angel told Pastor Daniel, *"If your record is to be called here, you will in no doubt be thrown into hell."* Pastor Daniel immediately defended himself saying, "I am a man of God! I serve Him with all my heart!" A Bible appeared in the angel's hand, and Pastor Daniel knew he was guilty for the angry words he had spoken to his wife. The angel also reminded him that *Jesus promised that God will not forgive our sins if we do not forgive others* (see Matt. 6:14-15), because we will reap what we have sown. Only those who are merciful will obtain mercy (see Matt. 5:7). The angel told Daniel that the prayers he prayed as he was dying in the hospital were of no effect, *because he refused to forgive his wife even when she attempted to reconcile* on the morning of his fatal accident.

Pastor Daniel wept. The angel told Daniel that the Lord was sending him back to be a witness to the penalty of unforgiveness.

Meanwhile, some believers gathered around Daniel's dead body and prayed. Suddenly Daniel sneezed and arose with a jump. He had been physically dead for almost two days when he came back to life.

Pastor Daniel Ekechukwu is now calling Christians to do what Christ has been commanding all His followers to do for two thousand years: *forgive one another!*

CAN UNFORGIVENESS ACTUALLY CAUSE A CHRISTIAN TO END UP IN HELL?

Scripture clearly and definitely answers Yes! Do you remember the parable Jesus told of the unforgiving servant found in Matthew 18:21-35? When the master learned that his servant, whom he had graciously forgiven, had refused to forgive a fellow servant, he was moved with anger and *"delivered him to the tormentors, till he should pay all that was due unto him"* (Matt. 18:24). The servant's formerly forgiven and unpayable debt was reinstated, so that he found himself once again owing what he could never repay. Jesus further warned, *"So likewise shall My heavenly Father do also unto you, if ye from your hearts forgive not every one his brother their trespasses"* (Matt 18:35).

CHRISTIANS CAN FORFEIT THEIR OWN SALVATION BY UNFORGIVENESS!

If you are among those who believe that once saved it is guaranteed that you will never face judgment for your own personal choices of unforgiveness, you may want to rethink your position. Often when it comes to the actual act of forgiving, we choose an opinion of man, whose message of forgiveness is meant only as a suggestion rather than a commandment. Many ministers these days seem to water down the message of forgiveness to a choice one may one day be willing to make. Do we really have a "choice" or time to delay? Forgive now before it is too late for you.

OFTEN WHEN IT COMES TO THE ACTUAL ACT OF FORGIVING, WE CHOOSE AN OPINION OF MAN, WHOSE MESSAGE OF FORGIVENESS IS MEANT ONLY AS A SUGGESTION RATHER THAN A COMMANDMENT.

Whenever you stand praying, forgive, if you have anything against anyone, so that your Father who is in heaven will also forgive you your transgressions. [But if you do not forgive, neither will your Father who is in heaven forgive your transgressions] (Mark 11:25-26 NASB).

The concept of unconditional forgiveness is so fundamental that Jesus taught its principles when He taught us to pray:

*Our Father which art in heaven, hallowed be Thy name. Thy kingdom come, Thy will be done in earth, as it is in heaven. Give us this day our daily bread. And **forgive us our debts, as we forgive our debtors.** And lead us not into temptation, but deliver us from evil: For Thine is the kingdom, and the power, and the glory, forever. Amen* (Matthew 6:9-13).

Jesus further emphasizes the key importance of forgiveness:

*For if ye forgive men their trespasses, your heavenly Father will also forgive you: But if ye forgive not men their trespasses, **neither will your Father forgive your trespasses*** (Matthew 6:14-15).

UNFORGIVENESS OPENS THE DOOR FOR DEMONIC OPPRESSION

The Word of God makes it clear that forgiveness is an absolute requirement for our own personal freedom. If we do not forgive others, God will not forgive us. God may also remove His protection from us, causing us to be turned over to the tormentors. I believe that the tormentors can come in many forms—from bodily illness to demonic activity. If we do not forgive, God allows the tormentor access to us (see Matt. 18:21-35).

One biblical meaning for *tormentor* in this passage is actually *a torturer.*[3] Webster's definition of *tormentor* is "one that torments."[4] To torment is "to inflict great physical pain or mental anguish. It also means a source of harassment, annoyance or pain. To agitate, upset greatly, pester or annoy."[5] It is hard to believe that simply through our unforgiveness we can legally open ourselves up to this degree of demonic harassment.

> *To whom ye forgive any thing, I forgive also: for if I forgave any thing, to whom I forgave it, for your sakes forgave I it in the person of Christ; lest Satan should get an advantage of us: for we are not ignorant of his devices* (2 Corinthians 2:10-11).

During my time as a prison chaplain, I have talked to hundreds of people who told me they struggle with the same bondages year after year. They beg God for breakthrough, yet they never see relief. I have discovered that in many cases personal bondages are linked to our unforgiveness.

In my course of ministry, I underwent a year-long training certification for the ability to minister deliverance and inner healing to wounded individuals and have been involved in the healing rooms. In case after case, the key to anyone's freedom was always his or her ability to forgive. Each session began and ended with that key point. When we would encounter an obstacle that prevented a receiver from receiving emotional or physical healing or deliverance, we would need to stop and re-evaluate if there was any unforgiveness, as it consistently was the open door the enemy used to invade someone's life.

One thing is certain, unforgiveness is one of satan's main devices in the weapon arsenal he uses against us. Strife, bitterness, resentment, gossip, and unforgiveness are significant tools he uses to keep us from inheriting the blessings of God.

The main reason satan doesn't want you to forgive (and he keeps reminding you of the pain) is that he knows your forgiveness will set you free to receive the fullness of everything God said you could have: miracles, blessings, victory, restoration, restitution, protection, reconciliation, anointing, ministry, increase, health, prosperity, and salvation (ours and others). Be assured, satan will do everything in his power to continually remind you of the offense, stirring the emotional (boiling) pot until he has fried you to a crisp and stolen your lunch money.

I believe those most targeted by the enemy are the same ones that the Lord desires to use greatly. Through your forgiveness, the Lord will pour a supernatural grace and favor that will catapult you into your destiny. Past your test is your testimony.

Unforgiveness Opens the Door for Physical Sickness

We have already established that forgiveness releases emotional healing, but do you know that many infirmities are rooted and established in unforgiveness? In fact unforgiveness is one reason why some people aren't healed. It gives the enemy an open door and legal right to attack their physical body. Many infirmities are linked to demonic activity. Unforgiveness opens the door to demonic warfare and enables a legal right for sickness within your body to manifest.

A study of 13,000 men and women who were unforgiving and angry, showed that they were three times as likely to have heart attacks or bypass surgery than individuals who were not. In cases of chronic pain, 60 percent of all chronic pain patients show a strong element of failure to forgive. In addition, people unwilling to forgive take an average of 25 percent more medication those who do forgive.[6]

In a national survey published in *The Journal of Adult Development* (2001), it was discovered that only 52 percent of Americans practice forgiveness. Of those, ages 45 and older were more likely to report having better overall mental and physical health than those who did not forgive.[7] A study in 2003 by Dr. Douglas Russell, a Veterans Administration Cardiologist, found that the coronary function of patients who had suffered a heart attack improved after a ten-hour course in forgiveness. He further stated that when anger is turned inward, bottled up, and directed at oneself, lack of forgiveness appears likely to have an ongoing, toxic health effect that may be even more corrosive to physical and mental health than anger directed outward. In the same study Dr. Russell discovered, forgiving women are three times less likely to suffer from depression.[8]

Professor Worthington of Virginia Commonwealth University found that people who won't forgive the wrongs committed against them tend to have negative indicators of health and well-being, more stress-related disorders, lower immune system functions, and worse rates of cardiovascular disease. In addition, unforgiving people experience higher rates of divorce.[9]

Dr. Guy Pettit's article, "Forgiveness and Health,"[10] links unforgiveness to many physical malfunctions:

Unforgiveness which often occurs as a result of having been hurt, humiliated, angered, or having suffered fear or loss, feelings of guilt, or envy, can have profound effects on the way your body functions. Muscles tighten, causing imbalances or pain in your neck, back, and limbs. Blood flow to the joint surfaces is decreased, making it more difficult for the blood to remove wastes from the tissues and reducing the supply of oxygen and nutrients to the cells. Normal processes of repair and recovery from injury or arthritis are impaired. Clenching of the jaws contributes to problems with teeth and jaw joints. Headaches are probable. Chronic pain may be worsened.

The list goes on: blood flow to the heart is constricted. Digestion is impaired. Breathing is restricted. The immune system functions less well, increasing vulnerability to infections and perhaps malignancy. Unforgiveness remains imprinted upon your nervous system.

ENDNOTES

1. Mary K. Baxter, *A Divine Revelation of Hell* (New Kensington, PA: Whitaker House, 1997), 54.

2. Excerpts of Pastor Daniel's story told by David Servant, "Concerning the Resurrection of Daniel Ekechukwu"; http://www .lit4ever.org/servant3.html (accessed May 14, 2009).

3. "Basanistes"; http://www.studylight.org/lex/grk/view.cgi ?number=930.

4. Merriam-Webster's Collegiate Dictionary, 11th ed., s.v. "Tormentor."

5. Merriam-Webster's Collegiate Dictionary, 11th ed., s.v. "Torment."

6. "The Health Benefits of Forgiveness"; http://www .forgivenessandhealth.com/html/benefits.html (accessed May 16, 2009).

7. *Journal of Adult Development,* October 2001, no. 8(4): 249-27.

8. Melissa Healy, "Forgive and Be Well?" http://articles .latimes.com/2007/dec/31/health/he-forgiveness31?pg=3 (accessed May 24, 2009).

9. Quoted in Gregg Easterbrook, "Forgiveness Is Good for Your Health"; http://www.iloveulove.com/forgiveness/forgivehealth.html (accessed May 24, 2009).

10. Dr. G.A. Pettitt, "Forgiveness and Health"; http://iloveulove .com/forgiveness/forgivhealth.htm (accessed May 24, 2009).

CHAPTER 17

THE MERITS OF FORGIVENESS

I have shared many reasons why we forgive throughout this book, both spiritually and physically. Some of the many reported benefits to forgiveness regarding your health include the following;

- Lower blood pressure

- Stress reduction

- Less hostility

- Better sleep

- Lower heart rate

- Lower incidents of alcohol or drug abuse

- Fewer depression symptoms

- Fewer anxiety symptoms

- Reduction of chronic pain

- Lower hypertension

- Removal of toxic emotions

- Lower incident of ulcers and digestive disorders

- Lower incident of eating disorders

- Overall feeling of well-being[1]

FORGIVENESS IS FREEING

To forgive is to set the prisoner free, and then you discover the prisoner was you!

Forgiveness sets you free to be all God designed you to be and do in the Kingdom. Forgiveness brings supernatural freedom as well as emotional and physical healing. Through forgiveness the Lord brings your feelings in line with your obedient decision to live by His Word. What's next? Blessings, restoration, reward, and overflow *to you!*

 *TO FORGIVE IS TO SET THE PRISONER FREE, AND THEN YOU DISCOVER THE PRISONER WAS YOU!*

Forgiveness means you choose God's way of healing and blessings instead of the world's way of hatred and death. This is the very nature of Jesus. He freely forgives you and requires your unconditional forgiveness—if you are going to be called by His name.

In this diagram you can see that the way of the cross, through forgiveness, is both horizontal and vertical.[2] On the horizontal bar are the words "I FORGIVE," which indicate our ability to reach out to others through our forgiveness. On the vertical bar, we see the words, "I AM FORGIVEN," indicating God reaching out to us with His forgiveness for us. Both bars are supernaturally linked, and one does not operate without the other. Forgiveness is the message of the cross. It is being strong enough to be Christ-like, which is truly a sign of real godly character and spiritual fruit. Forgiveness is trusting Jesus to handle your situation and heal the areas of your heart and life.

Forgiveness is the foundation of the Christian faith and the extraordinary heart of Jesus. His own example of unconditional love to us, through His death, is our key to successfully forgive others.

And be ye kind one to another, tenderhearted, forgiving one another, even as God for Christ's sake hath forgiven you (Ephesians 4:32).

Question: At what point is forgiveness necessary?

Answer: The minute you realize you have been offended!

Forgiveness is required as soon as you replay the negative situation or hurtful emotions repeatedly in your mind. Forgiveness is required when you secretly watch anticipating and, in some cases, even hoping that your offender will fall. Forgiveness is required if you watch for or take any secret delight when judgment comes to them. Ask the Holy Spirit to search your heart and reveal if you need to forgive anyone. His list might surprise you. I am always asking Him to reveal to me if I am harboring any degree of unforgiveness, bitterness, or offense. Then I strive to be quick to repent and forgive.

FORGIVENESS RELEASES A COMMANDED BLESSING

The act of forgiving is our seed of obedience to His Word. Once we have sown our seed, He is faithful to bring a bountiful harvest of blessings to us in every way possible.

Forgiveness brings internal peace and complete rest. Forgiveness brings salvation. Forgiveness brings healing and prosperity. Forgiveness brings relief and inner freedom. Forgiveness releases an open Heaven over your life. Psalm 133 speaks of the commanded blessing God releases when we live in unity.

> *Behold, how good and how pleasant it is for brethren to dwell together in unity! It is like the precious ointment upon the head, that ran down upon the beard, even Aaron's beard: that went down to the skirts of his garments; as the dew of Hermon, and as the dew that descended upon the mountains of Zion: for there the Lord commanded the blessing, even life for evermore* (Psalm 133:1-3).

God delights in turning what the enemy meant for evil into our good. He is a God of complete restoration because that is where His glory is the greatest. It is through our forgiveness of others that He has unrestricted access into our lives to restore beauty for ashes.

> *To give unto them beauty for ashes, the oil of joy for mourning, the garment of praise for the spirit of heaviness* (Isaiah 61:3).

> *Thou hast turned for me my mourning into dancing: Thou hast put off my sackcloth, and girded me with gladness* (Psalm 30:11).

A child of God, who operates under the love of Jesus and according to the laws of God and abides under the power of the Holy Spirit, will be willing to come to a place to forgive and release. We are all called to live our lives according to the character of Jesus and follow His example through the Word.

The Time to Repent Is Now!

It is indeed time for the Body of Christ to repent and pursue peace with all men.

If we expect God to forgive us, we must forgive others. That is what Jesus solemnly promised.

 *HEALING YOUR BROKEN HEART NOW BECOMES HIS RESPONSIBILITY AND HIS SPECIALTY!*

All Things Work Together for Good

OK, you have done the hardest part already by choosing to forgive and allowing the Holy Spirit to begin the process. The rest is up to the Holy Spirit. *Healing your broken heart now becomes His responsibility and His specialty!*

> *We know that all things work together for good to those who love God, to those who are the called according to His purpose* (Romans 8:28 NKJV).

> *Casting all your care upon Him; for He careth for you* (1 Peter 5:7).

I believe God is doing a quick work today to heal broken hearts and restore stolen lives, but immediate emotional healing may not always be the case. In some cases of severe woundedness and abuse, forgiveness is the *first step* toward total restoration. The Holy Spirit began restoring "things" back to me *immediately* once I made the decision to forgive, and eventually the complete healing of my heart did follow, but He made the journey very easy!

Be patient and tender with yourself. Know that the Lord wants you healed faster than you do so that He can open Heaven and pour out a blessing upon your head. Your breakthrough is on its way! All of Heaven is poised upon the Lord's command to pour out healing and restoration upon the hearts of those who turn and repent before the Lord. Draw near to Him, and see what Heaven has in store for *you*!

Your life and your pain are not insignificant to Him! Past your fear is your freedom! Past your fear is your destiny! Past your test is your testimony. Push past your circumstances and your fears to see the wonderful things God has in store for you. Dare to believe that the best is yet ahead. Dare to believe God's Word that He will make your latter years even greater than your former years.

> *Eye hath not seen, nor ear heard, neither have entered into the heart of man, the things which God hath prepared for them that love Him* (1 Corinthians 2:9).

With all the loss, death, sickness, testing, trials, and tribulations that Job suffered, the Lord blessed the latter days of Job more than his beginning because Job was faithful (see Job 42:12). God blesses faithfulness. God blesses forgiveness. God blesses every time we walk in obedience to His Word.

My staff and I have interceded for *you* that as you read this, the same Spirit of Restoration that blew across my face would gently blow across your face right now, bringing Heaven's sweet kiss to you too.

It is my prayer that you have been ministered to through my transparency, that as you have read the pages of my life, you now understand those same forgiveness steps the Holy Spirit took me through, and that it will be ever clear to you that our loving heavenly Father is *still* in control of your life. Despite everything the enemy tries to do to bring destruction, you too will be able to stand and say, *"If God is for me, who can stand against me?"* (see Rom. 8:31). *"Surely no weapon formed against me shall ever prosper"* (see Isa. 54:17).

> *But as for you, ye thought evil against me; but God meant it unto good, to bring to pass, as it is this day, to save much people alive* (Genesis 50:20).

> *Love your enemies, do good to them which hate you, bless them that curse you, and pray for them which despitefully use you* (Luke 6:27-28).

REMEMBER, THROUGH YOUR RESTORATION IS YOUR FATHER GREATLY PLEASED! (SELAH)

> *The Lord has taken away **your** judgments; He has cast out your enemy. The King of Israel, the Lord, is in your midst; you shall see disaster no more…The Lord your God in your midst, the Mighty One, will save; He will rejoice over you with gladness, He will quiet you with His love, He will rejoice over you with singing* (Zephaniah 3:15,17 NKJV).

SAMPLE FORGIVENESS PRAYERS[3]

These prayers may help you in getting started. Once you begin the wonderful healing journey of forgiveness, you will be amazed at its quick progress.

Prayer of Salvation

Isn't it a comfort to know that we can experience forgiveness in every area where we have sinned or blown it? There is nothing you have done that is too big for the Lord to heal and restore. If you have not asked Jesus into your heart, what better time is there than right now? It is so easy and not complicated because Jesus looks at our hearts. Open your heart now, and pray this prayer.

Dear Jesus,

I know You are the only Son of God. I know You came to this earth and died on the cross to save me. I know You rose from the dead. I ask You to forgive me of all my sins and cleanse me from all unrighteousness. I ask You to wash me with Your precious blood and to make me brand-new. I invite Your Holy Spirit into my life now. I renounce all ties with the enemy. Thank You for saving me. In Your name, Jesus, I pray. Amen.

Prayer for Forgiving Others

Father, You have said in Your Word that You desire for me to experience the healing and freedom that forgiveness brings. You require that I forgive so I can receive Your forgiveness. Therefore I choose to forgive

_____ *for* _____. *I refuse and renounce all thoughts of revenge, and I trust that in Your time You will deal with* _____ *as You see fit. I forgive all those who have set me up to enter into sin and all who have hurt me. I release them right now from any debt that I thought they owed me. I let go of all judgments and punishments that I personally have wanted them to receive. I receive Your power to forgive so that in my forgiving I can be set free. I turn every hurt, all pain, and these individuals over to You completely. In Jesus's name I pray. Amen.*

Prayer Asking God's Forgiveness

Father, now that I have forgiven all others, I come to You through the shed blood of Jesus and the power of His cross and ask You to forgive me for all of my sins. I acknowledge and take responsibility for each and every time I have violated Your commandments as well as for the sinful thoughts and plans that have been and are in my heart. By faith I apply the blood of Jesus to cover and cancel every curse established from my sin. Holy Spirit, I thank You for working forgiveness into my life, for healing me, and for cleansing me from all unrighteousness. Thank You, Father, for restoring me to fellowship with You. In the name of Jesus Christ my Lord and Savior. Amen.

Prayer for Forgiving Myself

Father, because You have forgiven me, I choose to forgive myself for all the ways I have hurt others out of my own hurt and pain, and the ways I have hurt myself. I choose to forgive and release myself from all accusations, judgments, hatred, and slander I have made against myself. I forgive myself for the mistakes, the stupidity, and other ways I have fallen short of the mark. I choose to accept myself as I am, because I know that You, Lord, love me, so I choose to begin to love myself. I know that You will not leave me in this condition, but You will draw me onward, freeing me from my current state. Holy Spirit, I give You permission to work Your work of sanctification in me. I embrace fully and look forward to You changing me into the image of Christ. In Jesus Christ's name I pray. Amen.

ENDNOTES

1. See http://www.mayoclinic.com/health/forgiveness/ MH00131 (accessed December 1, 2008).

2. The cross concept was taken from *Restoring the Foundations: An Intregrated Approach to Healing Ministry* by Chester and Betsy Klystra (Santa Rosa Beach, FL: Proclaiming His Word Publications, 2001), 98.

3. Chester and Betsy Klystra, *Restoring the Foundations: An Intregrated Approach to Healing Ministry* (Santa Rosa Beach, FL: Proclaiming His Word Publications, 2001).

CHAPTER 18

WHEN YOU BLAME GOD

I know that this chapter is straying a bit from the message of forgiveness, but I felt it was important to include in the end since I initially struggled with it myself. A portion of my unforgiveness was wrapped up in blaming God. Once I realized this, I tearfully repented. I pray it will bless someone.

Out of our own pain at times, we may question God's ability to adequately care for us. The enemy is constantly telling us that God does not care for us at all and that He has rejected us. In my case I felt God cared for others more than He cared about me, eventually even feeling God had hurt, betrayed, or abandoned me. I had a difficult time hearing His voice or receiving anything good from Him.

Often people who harbor anger and rejection feelings toward God may experience a hard time receiving anything emotionally or physically, particularly healing. In most cases and especially mine, disappointment with God became a trust issue resulting in an overall lack of trust in God and in His ability to care for and protect me.

The truth was that I made a poor choice to marry Jerry. In rebellion, I went against my mother's wishes in both dating and marrying him. I had been a very rebellious teenager and felt that I alone knew what was best for my life. I did not follow God's Word for choosing a mate, and when I married, we were worlds apart and completely unequally yoked, desiring different goals. Shortly after the marriage, I repented for my rebellious lifestyle and made every attempt to live a godly life, but I was then trusting God to intervene and change the choices I made through rebellion.

Anger toward God is a common feeling for someone who has been severely wounded. Many devoutly serious Christians have struggled with feelings of rejection from God from time to time.

You too may think, *"Why would the one who allowed hurt to come to me want to now come heal me?"* Often these emotions can lead you to feel that God does not care about you. Sometimes this belief can block you from hearing God's voice, since the ability to hear God's voice greatly increases the effectiveness of receiving healing.

Unfortunately, some churches teach that it is sacrilegious, ungodly, and, yes, even dangerous to be disappointed toward God. As a result, attempting to work through real negative feelings is seen as a lack of faith, weakness, or rebellion. Often someone disappointed with God feels that to admit anger toward God is scary to look at or too shameful to acknowledge.

I ultimately felt that God would be angry with me and punish me for having and expressing these real feelings of hatred that I had toward Him.

The Lord began to teach me that trust is love. *Love is the foundation of trust. Trust is bound by love and empowered by love.* Because God loves me, I can trust Him to guide my life. Scripture teaches us that we were created in love, because of love, and by love. It shows us that Jesus loved us before we were created and before we even found salvation in Him. Learning to trust the Lord is learning to trust in His ability to love us. Once you confidently begin to trust the written Word of God, which teaches throughout about God's love for you, negative trust or abandonment issues will quickly fade away. When we are secure in our understanding of how much God loves us, we can be secure in our trust of Him.

It is OK to admit that you have blamed God, but don't stop there. Be willing to deal with your own sins and the consequences they played in your life and move on. We all make poor choices at times. Acknowledge your feelings of blame and repent to God. He loves you in spite of your blame and wants to heal your life if you will ask Him to. Put the blame where it really belongs—on the devil. Remember satan comes to steal, kill, and destroy, but God gives life abundantly.

If you are disappointed and feel that the Lord may have rejected or abandoned you, this prayer may help you:

Dear Lord,

I see that I have misjudged You and blamed You for things You did not do. I choose today to stop doing this.

199

I ask You to forgive me for my sin against You of blaming You for every negative circumstance in my life. I know and affirm that You love me, that You are a good God, and that You want only the best for me, which is to conform me into the image of Jesus Christ.

I agree with You that You are in charge of my life and that You are using everything that happens to me for my development into a son/daughter able to rule and reign with You in eternity.

I will put the blame where it really belongs, on myself (for my own poor choices) and satan. I will stop being a blame shifter but will be responsible for my own life under the guidance and control of the Holy Spirit. I choose to trust Your work in my life because You love me.

Thank You, Lord, for new trust today, and for a renewed relationship with You. I receive both of these in the name of Jesus Christ. Amen. [1]

ENDNOTE

1. Chester and Betsy Klystra, *Restoring the Foundations: An Intregrated Approach to Healing Ministry* (Santa Rosa Beach, FL: Proclaiming His Word Publications, 2001), 215.

CONCLUSION

IT'S YOUR TURN!

Blessed are they that mourn: for they shall be comforted
(Matthew 5:4).

I hear the Spirit of the Lord saying in this season: "It is your turn to rise above that which has tried to destroy your life; that which has attempted to steal the very essence of life from you, from who you are, and from what you will be."

You may have walked through some seriously difficult things in your life over which you had little control, but He encourages that it is a new season for you. Old things have passed away and all things have become new, or will become new for you (see 2 Cor. 5:17).

Ecclesiastes 3:1-8 reminds us that for everything in life there are seasons, appointed times, and time limits. Whatever the enemy attempts to bring against you has an appointed time limit. Even crying and weeping has a time limit. The Bible says in Psalm 30:5 that we cry through the night, but joy comes in the morning. As long as you have been alive, morning has always come. At difficult times in your life, it may seem that morning will never come for you, but according to God's law of seasons, it must come eventually.

They that sow in tears shall reap in joy (Psalm 126:5).

Oh what unspeakable joy when morning does come! So let me encourage you. Throughout your life there are many seasons, and the place you are now is not the place you will be next year. If things are rocky now, just hang on. They must change when you put your trust in the Lord.

Ronda Brown (living out Isaiah 54)
Dunamis Power Ministries

APPENDIX

PERSONAL PROPHESIES

I wanted to include these personal prophecies because they offered such hope to me, and they show the Father's heart to restore, to bless, and to heal. It is quite apparent that God had a handle on my life, a plan, purpose, and destiny. Outside of the arena of the conference I volunteered at, Stacy Campbell did not know me, and had no knowledge of my history; yet, she faithfully delivered a true word of the Lord for me when I needed it most. He has a word and a destiny for you too. Ask Him for it.

DELIVERED THROUGH STACEY CAMPBELL

RevivalNOW! Ministries

www.RevivalNow.com

January 8, 2006

Father, I just want to bless Ronda. And I just see such passion and desire for God....

And God has really blessed you. I feel like for some things in your life that you have gone through a real trauma in your past, and you thought things were over and, you know, but God had a future for you and a hope and then He opened up a whole new future that is so restorative. I feel like the restoration of God in every realm, in the financial realm, in the spiritual blessing realm, and in the favor realm and just favor with people and God. And God has so blessed you. And I feel like there was a time...maybe that is why you are so childlike...it is like all things are new to you now. Because of what you went through in the past it feels like really dark, really black and there was a season of that. And you thought that the light and the new dawn would never come, but when it did you are so grateful.

It's like a kid who never had something before, and now they got something; they never experienced it before, and they are so grateful for it. And the experience is, "I can't believe it. I can't believe it." And there is a gratitude to God and this thankful heart that you have and this desire for God, and God just wants to fill it over and over and over again.

And so I see into your future. I see God raising you up, and I see if you want to be great in God's Kingdom you have to be a servant of all. And the open door for you is going to be servanthood, and as you serve you are going to be elevated and elevated.

And I see meetings and you praying for people and the power of God just shooting through you. Do you do that already? And He is just adding things. I see Him adding.

And I see the prophetic. I see the whole prophetic realm opening up to you more and more and more. I see a new increase, especially when you lay hands on them and suddenly you will have a word of knowledge. I pray impartation. Great Impartation for that word of knowledge that she would even see more, more history, more details, more future, all this whole thing. Lord, we just pray impartation of the prophetic. Stir up in her the desire to earnestly seek prophetic gifts.

And she's done that—she's so hungry, Lord. She's so wanted more and more of the revelation of You and the revelation of the supernatural. And I feel out of the revelation and out of the supernatural realm and out of the word of knowledge will come healing and the gifts of healing. And suddenly you will just start praying for the sick and emotional healing and then physical healing. All these different things and He's just adding and adding and adding to you.

And it's like every new thing, every new gifting. It's like you say, *"Oh, new fun thing!!!"* You know? And it's like just the joy of God as a child in the Kingdom of Heaven. I just feel to say to you, "The sky's the limit!" That as you are faithful in the small, God is going to make you faithful over many things.

So don't let your history dictate your future. And what I feel God meant by that is that there are mindsets maybe that came from your history, that you have developed mindsets, that you have said this far but no farther. But the Lord wants to say the sky is the limit. And don't ever think, "God, I've had enough. It's over the top. I just can't have any more, because that would be too much." But the Lord says, "Exceedingly abundantly."

I see you on stages. I see you giving your testimony. I see the Lord doing so many things from you that you would never ever have thought.

And so you will be one that just tastes and sees and the then tells about the goodness of God. And so, Lord, we just bless that. I just see in all these things, Ronda, you are just a joy giver. Amen.

ANOTHER PROPHETIC WORD

May 2008

My beautiful daughter, you are so dear to My heart. At one time the enemy tried to convince you that you were just a piece of coal. But even then I saw you as a diamond in the rough. I've since taken that precious stone, and I've carved off all the edges, and I've cut you into a beautiful diamond in My crown.

You are a rare jewel that some notice in an instant—those who have eyes to see. Others may not see right away, though when they walk away they know that they've experienced something out of the ordinary.

Many are called, but few are chosen. I have chosen you from the beginning, and as you walk in Me, people will see Me in you. You will draw them with love, as I have loved you. So shine, My lovely, and know that you are special to Me and you always have been.

My love for you [Ronda] is never-ending.

BOOKINGS

To book Ronda Brown as a guest speaker, contact

DUNAMIS POWER MINISTRIES
E-mail: dunamispower3@gmail.com
Or visit us on the web at www.DunamisPower.com.

Re-Nue Herbal Formulas

To order the same herbal formulas the Lord gave to Ronda go to www.Re-Nue.com.

ABOUT THE AUTHOR

Ronda Brown owned and operated her own thriving alternative medicine company for many years until the Lord asked her to lay it down in exchange for a miracle-working ministry. An accomplished writer and speaker, she has lectured and ministered internationally and from coast-to-coast within the continental United States She has done extensive work in radio, and co-hosted weekly live radio programs. A prison chaplain for three years, she is also trained and certified to minister deliverance. She founded "Dunamis Power Ministries," based in East Houston, Texas. An ordained minister, Ronda operates under an open Heaven with numerous signs and wonders following. Supernatural creative miracles are an everyday part of her life.

The Lord has used her mightily to witness broken and deformed bodies powerfully restored. She operates under a sharp prophetic mantle, keenly calling out specific words of knowledge that catapults the receiver into their breakthrough. She has a heart for the lost, the brokenhearted, the neglected, and the abandoned.

Through her transparency and dedication, it is her hope that you too will discover the unspeakable joys of living an obedient life, holy and pleasing to the Master, and that your steps into ministry will be shortened as you journey down the roadmap the Lord gave her to follow.

Ronda currently resides in East Houston, Texas, with her (way too much attitude) Chihuahua, Spartacus AKA: Sparky. She is the mother of two beautiful daughters and grandmother to one young grandson.

FORTHCOMING BOOKS BY DUNAMIS POWER MINISTRIES

Face to Face by Ronda Brown

During Ronda's long transition from secular business into full-time ministry, the Lord powerfully met with her regularly and gave her prophetic directives to shorten her ministry preparation and powerfully equip her ministry to new levels. Each visit would reveal another nugget necessary for her victorious new life. As He spoke each word, she would transcribe them in her journals. She has shared each nugget in this book. Within *Face to Face* are insights into the operating mind of Christ and functions of ministry. You too will be utterly amazed as each letter draws you into the deep waters where the mysteries of God flow abundantly, challenging you to the level of supernatural spiritual growth of which you have always dreamed.